Going 1

A Play

John Godber

A SAMUEL FRENCH ACTING EDITION

SAMUEL FRENCH

FOUNDED 1830

SAMUELFRENCH-LONDON.CO.UK
SAMUELFRENCH.COM

FOR AMATEUR PRODUCTION ENQUIRIES

UNITED KINGDOM AND WORLD EXCLUDING NORTH AMERICA

plays@SamuelFrench-London.co.uk

020 7255 4302/01

Each title is subject to availability from Samuel French,

depending upon country of performance.

GOING DUTCH

First performed in December 2004 at the Hull Truck
Theatre, Spring Street, Hull, with the following cast:

Mark	Jimmy Hornsby
Sally	Gemma Craven
Gill	Jackie Lye
Karl	Rob Hudson
Crooner	Rob Hudson

Directed by John Godber
Designed by Pip Leckonby

CHARACTERS

Mark, composer, 52
Sally, his wife, 52
Gill, a friend from university days, 47
Karl, a beast, 48
A Singer, 40

SYNOPSIS OF SCENES

The action of the play takes place on a cross-channel liner and in various parts of Amsterdam.

Time — the present

Other plays by John Godber published by
Samuel French Ltd

April In Paris
Blood Sweat and Tears
Departures
Gym and Tonic
Happy Families
It Started With a Kiss
Lucky Sods
Men of the World
Passion Killers
Perfect Pitch
Salt of the Earth
Teechers
Unleashed
Up 'n' Under
Up 'n' Under II
Weekend Breaks

ACT I
SCENE 1

The set is essentially an open space which can transform itself into a multitude of different locations. We need to have the sense of a very expensive luxury cruise liner, but we also have to create levels of disco mania which happen on the lower decks. Spotlights are used to isolate the action and to pinpoint various locations on the ship

When the play begins, the stage is in darkness. There is a small round table on stage with two chairs by it. The singer — smartly dressed in distressed black tie — stands nearby, unlit as yet

Music plays; the introduction to Neil Diamond's "Hello Again"

The Lights fade up, creating the Sky Lounge

Mark and Sally enter. During the following dialogue they move to the chairs and sit

Mark (*to the audience*) So here we are.
Sally (*to the audience*) Nice and settled.
Mark Sat up in the Sky Lounge
Sally On the *Pride of Hull*.
Mark It's a quarter to twelve.
Sally There's only us here.
Mark And a crooner is singing Neil Diamond!

A single spotlight picks out the singer. He sings "Hello Again"

The song finishes and a music track plays under the following

Singer (*speaking*) Ladies and gentlemen, I hope you have a great crossing this evening. It's been a pleasure working for you! The sea is slight, there's no wind and you should have a very relaxing night. Thank you very much and I'll be with you later!

Mark and Sally politely applaud

The spotlight on the singer fades out and he exits

The suggestion of a piano track can be heard underneath the following

Sally (*to Mark*) He's good actually.
Mark (*to Sally*) They work him hard though.
Sally How do you know?
Mark He's got to go down to the disco for the Freddie Mercury set now!
Sally How do you know?
Mark I've seen him do it. He did the same the last time we were on. You were too drunk to notice!
Sally (*to the audience; with the relaxed air of conversation*) We're going to the Christmas markets in Amsterdam!
Mark (*to the audience*) Probably come back with some rubbish!
Sally Get some tulips!
Mark Stuff for the tree.
Sally Nice stuff!
Mark You can get the same in Aldi's but — —
Sally It's not the same!
Mark Same price though!

A beat

Sally We're just past the end of England. You know; that sharp bit.
Mark That bit that Alan Titsmarsh says has got more birds on it than any other part of England. I don't know how he knows that, but ...
Sally We're sailing towards Euro-port!
Mark Ten square miles of oil pipes.
Sally You wake up and it's like you've died and gone to BP heaven.
Mark We don't get away much together.
Sally But we're making the effort! You've got to!
Mark We get on the boat at half seven, and the next morning we're there. Mind you I never sleep!
Sally It's his age.
Mark I can't sleep anywhere. I'm getting like my dad.
Sally You snore like your dad!
Mark How do you know?
Sally Well...
Mark It could be worse, I could be getting like your dad.
Sally Bless him!
Mark Silly old sod!

A beat

Sally You have to treat yourself, you know. Life's too short!
Mark Fifty-two now! Never thought I'd make fifty!

A beat

Sally I never thought people actually wore sleep masks, but ...
Mark That's supposed to be funny!
Sally And headphones to sleep in!
Mark Here we go!
Sally And take herbal sleeping pills.
Mark I'll try anything!
Sally When he goes to bed, it looks like he's going to the electric chair!

A beat

Mark This is what it's like, living in a house full of women.
Sally We've got three girls.
Mark Hell on earth!
Sally He's just bought himself a sun house for the garden.
Mark To live in!

A beat

Sally And that's another thing we swore we'd never do: private education, but ...
Mark It's not a dress rehearsal is it?
Sally I've been saying that for years and now the penny's dropped.
Mark I've voted Labour all my life but ... And now they've got this gambling thing. Dumbing down, the country's drowning in ignorance! That's why we stay in the Sky Lounge.
Sally Yes, there's usually a stag night on board, isn't there?
Mark And they're not going for the tulips!

A beat

Sally We go whenever we can now!
Mark That's ever since we went with Gill, isn't it?
Sally It was his fiftieth!
Mark Springsteen was touring Europe.
Sally He'd always had his eye on Gill to be honest!

Mark I only offered to help out if she ever got desperate.

Sally We were at University together! And he was always all over her like a rash!

Mark I was, I admit it, I was pathetic!

A beat

Sally We'd got this idea, that if ever Springsteen came near, we'd go and see him!

Mark Well, he'd helped the Yorkshire miners during the strike, don't know if you know that? And music's my thing, so it was my birthday treat — that's how my family works you see, you have to treat yourself!

A beat

Sally He thought he was going to get lucky! Especially since the gig was in Amsterdam!

Mark Well, it did cross my mind! It was perfect, you see: they could go on a spree, and I'd drift around the red light district for six hours window-shopping!

Sally I got my mum and dad over to house-sit. Keep their eye on the girls!

Mark Her dad insisted on re-wiring the house for something to do!

Sally He thinks that's funny!

Mark Re-plant a few trees, do a loft conversion,you know what these eighty-year olds are like!

Sally The thing about Gill is she's great
company though, isn't she?

Mark And she's godmother to our eldest.

Sally She hasn't got two pennies to scratch her bits with — but she is sexy isn't she?

Mark Well, I think so! But I've been wrong before, look at you.

A beat

Sally We were sat up here weren't we?

Mark And then in she came — like a whirlwind!

Gill enters US. *She is a vivacious and curvy forty-seven year-old who is showing far too much cleavage for her own good*

Gill I've been looking all over the bloody boat for you! I thought you'd

be down in the disco. What you doing up here in the posh bit? You've
got to be dead to like it up here, haven't you? (*She freezes*)
Sally We hadn't seen her for six months!
Mark But that's what she's like ...
Sally You don't see her for ages and then you just pick it up again!
Gill (*unfreezing*) Hiya, darling, how you doing?

*Gill joins Sally and Mark. There is much hugging and kissing. There
is much excited laughing. The characters talk to each other from this
point*

Sally All right?
Gill Yes are you?
Mark You're looking good, kid.
Gill Oh hallo, what's he after?

They share a laugh

Sally Your body!
Gill As usual!
Mark Never say never!

Sally considers Gill

Sally You look brilliant!
Gill Who?
Sally You!
Gill I don't, you do!

A beat

Mark We waited but we had to get the car on. You got your ticket?
Gill Yes, I've got all my stuff. Bloody rush to get here but ... I'm in
cabin 8101.
Sally Next to us.
Gill It's big, isn't it?
Mark The cabin or the boat?
Gill The boat, you drip!
Mark Because our cabin isn't!
Sally Well they're only for sleeping in really!
Gill I'll probably be pissed up anyway, so ... !
Mark (*getting up and heading for the exit*) You'll not be by yourself,
half the boat are legless before we leave the dock. Do you want a
drink?

Gill Can I get a pint?

Mark Hey, we're on a for a long time, you know?

Gill Fourteen hours. And it's going to get rough according to … Who is it?

Sally Who?

Gill The driver! Can't resist a man in uniform.

Mark I'll remember that!

Gill I saw him when I got on. Anyway, how's your mum?

Mark Oh, up and down!

Sally She's all right at the moment!

Gill How's your dad?

Sally Still moaning.

A round of laughter

Gill Must be all right then!

Sally (*considering Gill*) Have you lost weight?

Gill Six pounds.

Sally Oh!

Gill (*smugly showing off*) I'm sorry. The Atkins.

Sally Oh, impressed!

Mark I tried that — gave me the wind and sent my cholesterol up.

Gill What is he like?

Sally He's like a man only more stupid.

Gill I thought he was!

A round of laughter

Mark She's funny, you know!

Gill I know that.

Mark She wasn't then, but she can be!

A round of laughter

Gill I can't believe we're actually doing something we said we would.

Sally It's taken us thirty years, but — — !

Mark Hey, "Tramps like us … "

Gill "Baby we were born to run!"

Sally Except he can't; he's got bad knees.

A round of laughter

Mark I am bloody fifty! That's just insane!

Gill I know what I'm getting you for your birthday anyway!
Mark This is my present — us three together!
Gill Oh, he's full of shit, isn't he?
Sally Right up to the top!

A round of laughter

Gill Listen, can I just pop back to the cabin and get sorted — do you mind? I'll only be half an hour! I want to get some perfume and stuff. I've come without a lot of things. I'll see you in a bit — is that all right?

Gill exits

Silence

Mark Bloody Gill?
Sally Ohh!
Mark What was she wearing, though?
Sally Maybe she was looking for work when we got there?
Mark I think she'd got a chance dressed like that!
Sally Well, she'd got you as a client for a start.
Mark Hey, she's a bit picky — she's turned me down twice!

Sally turns to the audience

Sally (*to the audience*) She'd had some bad luck with men!
Mark (*to the audience*) We'd tried to fix her up but ... !
Sally There was Alan and Danny, wasn't there?
Mark She hated Danny, though, didn't she?
Sally And Alan was gay.
Mark So that was mistake!
Sally We didn't know, did we?
Mark No! And I don't think Alan knew for sure!

A beat

Sally Anyway I stayed in the Sky Lounge and he went for a walk around the ship, didn't you? That's what he does, he just leaves me and walks about, he says just thinking. Comes back an hour later with some daft idea usually!

During the following, Mark pulls a small truck carrying the setting for Scene 2 — the sun deck — on to the stage, then moves around the stage helping to set up the next scene

Mark That's it, I just had a float about, didn't I? I went down on to the sun deck. And I saw Gill; she was stood at the back here, smoking! I never think of her as a smoker, but I tell you, even after thirty years she still looked great to me!

Piano music plays as if from the Sky Lounge

Gill enters the sun deck area

Scene 2

The Sun Deck

The Lights cross-fade to the sun deck. Gill is looking out towards the dock in Hull. She lights a cigarette and takes a few big dramatic draws on it

Mark comes to the area where Gill is standing. Their manner is friendly but slightly loaded. They stand in silence for a while

Sally remains sitting in the Sky Lounge area and watches the scene

Mark All right?
Gill Calm, isn't it?

A beat

Mark Well, we're still in Hull you know! We haven't set off yet!
Gill I know that, you drip! (*She smokes and blows out heavily*) Fifty, then!
Mark Oph!

A beat

Gill Nice cabins!
Mark I hope I don't pick the wrong one when I turn in.
Gill Ay, you'd get a shock then!
Mark So would you!
Gill Do you think so?

A beat

Mark Wouldn't be that bad, would it?

Gill What would Sal say?

A beat

Mark I can just see me getting too drunk to know where I am and then coming in and snuggling up!

A beat

Gill And me being sick all over you!
Mark It'd be a genuine mistake though.
Gill In your dreams, mate!
Mark I've been dreaming that for thirty years!

A beat

Gill How's work going?
Mark Can't finish this bloody thing I'm doing.
Gill What is it?
Mark It's a kids series, can you believe it? I thought I'd be Philip Glass and I'm doing the background music on some Teletubbies bollocks!
Gill At least it's work.
Mark It's not art though.
Gill Who's bothered? (*She draws heavily on her cigarette*)
Mark How's it going then?
Gill Work or what?
Mark Or what?

A beat

Gill Work's shit. I've been a banana woman, I've been on perfume in John Lewis. And I've been a nanny, you should try that!
Mark I've been a nanny for the last twelve years.
Gill I've sacked my agent!
Mark Good for you!
Gill It was only a matter of time before she sacked me anyway.
Mark Get your retaliation in first!
Gill I've been doing prison workshops for the last three months!
Mark That's a bit real for me!
Gill Fascinating, though! Unbelievable, some of those blokes!
Mark I bet.

A beat

Gill You all right then?

Mark (*betraying some dissatisfaction; awkwardly*) I dunno!

Gill Why?

Mark My mother's been off it, in and out of hospital. My dad's knackered. Work! Girls are growing up! Sally's up and down, like I don't know what! Hormones or something! Sometimes you want to run away!

Gill No, I've done that — it's shit!

Mark smiles and laughs. He is very fond of Gill

Mark You!

Gill What?

Mark You're funny. (*He goes to kiss her*)

Gill Don't kiss me!

Mark (*a little taken aback*) I was only ...

Gill Please!

Mark Sally's in the bar.

Gill Mark?

Mark Hey, it's only ... !

Gill I know, but...

Mark Oh right!

A beat

Gill It's been a near miss, let's keep it like that!

Mark You look great!

Gill I look cheap but ——

Mark Give up! (*He turns away, slightly embarrassed*)

Gill Going to get rough, then?

Mark That's what the sick bags are for. When they line the corridors it's a giveaway!

A beat

Gill You look great!

Mark For fifty?

Gill I think you're getting better looking!

Mark It's your eyesight man, it's getting worse!

Gill Probably.

A round of laughter

Mark Listen, I've booked a table in the *Quatre Saisons* for nine-thirty
— is that ... ?
Gill Is that the posh one?
Mark It's all taken care of, so no questions ... If I can't kiss you at least
I can treat you! (*He senses dissent*) Why don't you ... ?
Gill I don't know if it's me, to be honest.
Mark Course it is!
Gill I just feel a bit ...
Mark What?

A beat

Gill I know it's good of you to pay for me, but ...
Mark Hey, we're mates, aren't we? You've got to let me do things for
you!
Gill Yes, but mates don't usually want to shag each other!
Mark That depends what kind of mates you've got!

A beat

Gill Well I don't want to shag you, let's just say that!

A beat

Mark Why do you always say the wrong things?
Gill Habit of a lifetime?

A beat

Mark Come on, I'll buy you that pint. If it's going to get rough we'll
sleep through it! And listen, don't know where you've got the idea that
I'd like to shag you from!
Gill No, that's right!

Mark and Gill share a friendly laugh

Gill exits US

Mark So we didn't eat in *Quatre Saisons* which is the *à la carte*. We
ate in the Four Seasons buffet, where you can go back as many times
as you like! I call it the "Trough Bar" because people stuff themselves
like animals. I saw a group of Dutch kids go back thirteen times.
Unlucky for some, they were going to see that again! After dinner and

a bit of shopping we returned to the Sky Lounge, where the singer was
doing his Neil Diamond set. He was really good actually! Or was it me
lowering my standards?

Mark strikes the sun deck truck, then exits

SCENE 3

Sky Lounge

The Lights cross-fade back to the Sky Lounge

*Music plays; the introduction to Neil Diamond's "Girl, You'll Be a
Woman Soon"*

The singer enters, dressed as before and as yet unlit

 Gill enters and joins Sally at the table, as yet unlit

*A spotlight picks out the singer in the Sky Lounge. He sings Neil
Diamond's "Girl, You'll Be a Woman Soon"*

The song finishes

Singer (*speaking*) Ladies and gentlemen, That's all from me for the
moment! I hope you have a great time in the Sky Lounge and on the
Pride of Hull! And although we're sailing into a gale force ten, I hope
it won't mar your enjoyment of the evening's entertainment … I'll be
back later with songs from the shows! Thank you!

 The Lights go down on the singer and he exits

Music plays under the rest of the scene without a lyric track

*The Lights come up on the table where Sally and Gill are sitting. They
are having a good time*

Mark arrives with drinks

Sally We could have eaten in the posh one you know.

Mark delivers the drinks

Gill I know, but I like going back for more! I felt like Oliver!

Mark We saw that, you must have gone up to the beef thirty times.
Gill Not thirty! Ten!
Mark Eight, I counted.
Gill What is he like?

A beat

Sally Did he tell you we've taken the plunge, we're sending Carla and
Beatrice private next year.
Gill You never ... ?
Sally I know! I know!
Mark Listen when a mate who's Head of the NUT for the South East
says, "If you've got the money, do it," it's good enough for me!

They all roll a little

Mark Like the man said.
Gill Getting choppy.
Mark Freezing outside and all!
Sally Did I ever tell you about coming on here with Radio
Humberside?
Mark Oh listen to this!
Sally I was helping on a listeners' trip!
Mark This is about five months ago, isn't it?
Sally They wanted to do a programme from the ship!
Mark A "Dutch Dash"; there and back in one day.
Sally Who's telling this story?
Mark Go on!
Sally It's a gale force thirty or something, and we're coming up the
Humber — it's so bad we couldn't dock!
Mark They're stuck at the mouth of the river.
Sally Everything's all over the place. Plates, everything!
Mark I'm listening to the radio.
Sally They were supposed to be doing the *Morning Tide* programme.
Had this new DJ — says he can handle the boat. Anyway, he's sat at
the mike and he says: "Hallo, welcome to Morning purph, this is Steve
oph, from Radio Uphm!"
Mark There's a good half-hour of him throwing up on air! Now that's
good radio!
Sally There's two old women; they're the only two who aren't sick on
the entire boat. I says, "Aren't you ill?" They said, "No, we're fine!" I
said, "Have you ever been on the boat before?" They say we've never
been to sea before; but we're from fishing stock!

Mark They'd gone to see Tony Bennett, hadn't they? They didn't realize they weren't staying, they were coming back the same night!

Sally Honestly funny!

Mark I've had a thought. I need to nip back down to the shop. (*He stands, then sways as if responding to the boat moving*) Oh, oh, here we go! You don't notice till you stand up. I'm going to get a plug adapter, I've come without one for my phone. I want to keep it charged. Might treat myself to a fridge magnet and all.

Sally Another?

Mark You can't have too many. See you in a bit.

Mark makes his way us. *He has to struggle a little as if the boat is swaying*

Sally and Gill freeze

So I left them to catch up, and have a wander around the boat. Down in the Sunset lounge the disco was about to start and the singer from the Sky Lounge was doing his Freddie Mercury. Let's just put it like this, he was better as Neil Diamond.

Mark moves further us, *reacting to the rocking and tilting of the boat*

Sally and Gill break from their freeze

Gill What's he like?

Sally A bloody nightmare most of the time!

A beat

Gill I can't believe he's fifty!

Sally Neither can he!

Gill Where's it gone?

A beat

Sally Are you OK then?

Gill Me? Yes! Why?

Sally Just wondered!

A beat

Gill No, no!

Sally Actually you can just feel it rock can't you?

A beat

Gill Well, actually, Sal ...

A beat

I feel awful, to be honest.
Sally Well, have a rum and Coke, that's supposed to settle you!
Gill It's not that!
Sally What is it, then?
Gill (*embarrassed and frustrated with herself*) Oh God!
Sally What?
Gill Oh hell, what am I bloody like? You're my best mate, for God's sake.
Sally What, tell me then!
Gill I feel like a bloody teenager!
Sally What is it?
Gill Can't we wait while Mark comes back?
Sally Why, is it about Mark?
Gill No, but ...
Sally What?

A beat

Gill Oh hell!
Sally What?

A beat

Gill I've — found somebody.
Sally (*delighted for Gill*) What?
Gill I know!
Sally Argh!
Gill Exactly!
Sally Arghhh!
Gill Shhh!
Gill I know.
Sally When?
Gill A couple of months!
Sally Why didn't you ... ?
Gill I don't know!
Sally I mean how? Where?

Gill Oh, don't, I'm still not a hundred percent but ...
Sally Didn't you want to tell us?
Gill I wanted to tell you and Mark at the same time.
Sally And is he?
Gill What?
Sally What's he like?
Gill Oph!
Sally What?
Gill Oh yeh.
Sally What?
Gill Oph!
Sally Yes?

The two women giggle wildly

Gill Oh yes!
Sally I can't believe it!
Gill (*jokily threatening*) What do you mean by that?
Sally I mean, it's great!
Gill It is!

A beat

Sally And is it the whole, you know the whole thing? The whole hog?
Gill It is the whole roasted hog, I'm afraid.
Sally I can't bear it, it's excellent!
Gill The whole stuffed roasted hog on a spit!
Sally (*gleefully excited*) Oh hell!
Gill I know.
Sally Oh brilliant!
Gill Forty-seven years and suddenly I'm eighteen!
Sally You lucky sod!
Gill I know!

A beat

Sally How did it?
Gill Just weird, but when I met him I just knew. I mean he's been divorced and there's baggage but ...
Sally Hey, we're not kids!
Gill Exactly!
Sally There's bound to be.

Mark returns DS. *He is still swaying as if the boat rocks gently*

Mark Can't charge my bloody phone up now. (*He sits. Sensing something*) What's up now, then?
Sally What?
Mark There's something, I don't know what it is, but ... !
Sally Gill's got something to tell you!
Mark What, she doesn't want to come? A bit late — we're in the middle of the North Sea!
Sally It's not that!
Mark Is it worse?

A beat

Sally She's got a fella.

Silence

Mark It's not gay Alan, is it?
Gill (*slightly hurt but playing against it*) This is serious, you arse!
Mark It was serious for Alan!
Gill What is he like honestly?

A beat

Sally Gill is in love, you pillock!
Gill Well, I wouldn't say that just yet!
Mark (*slightly hurt*) Well, brilliant! Great! (*He goes to kiss Gill*)

Gill lets him kiss her

Sally You can't do that now!
Gill Absolutely!
Sally You pleased for her?
Mark Why didn't you ... ?
Gill I felt about sixteen when I told Sal, so ... !
Mark I mean, great!
Gill It's been a whirlwind.
Mark Well, who is it? Do we know him or ... ?
Gill You don't know him!
Mark Does he have a name then or ... ?

A beat

Gill Karl.
Sally Karl!
Mark Karl!

A beat

Sally She's playing it cagey!
Mark Karl ... mmm!
Sally Why didn't you tell us as soon as you saw us?
Gill I couldn't.
Sally Why not?
Gill Because I thought you would have gone mad!
Sally Why?

A beat

Gill Because he's come with me!

A big silence

Sally Great!

A beat

Gill I mean, I can't believe I've asked him but ...

A beat

Mark Oh right, well, great!
Gill He says he'll pay for the cabin and everything. That's why I went
   down to ask. I just wanted to be straight. I know how good you've
   been to me. And he didn't want to eat in the posh bit, so I suggested
   we had the buffet but then he fell asleep ... !

A beat

Mark But has he got a ticket for the concert or ...
Gill He was going anyway!

A beat

Mark Oh right!

A beat

Gill He's a massive Springsteen fan!

A beat

Mark Oh well. That's excellent, then.
Sally Where is he?
Gill He's crashed out. He says he'll get a shower and meet us down the
   Irish Bar.
Mark He's Irish then?
Gill (*gathering her confidence*) No, but he likes a drink!
Mark So we're going to go down to the Irish bar?
Gill He says he'll see us in there!
Mark Why don't you get him to come up here?
Gill He hates it up here!
Mark Well, at least we can chat!
Gill He hates it though!
Mark Get him to come up here, it'll be a lot better.
Gill It's not us though, really...
Mark Well, ay, but ...
Sally We'll go down to the Irish bar! It'll be a laugh!
Mark (*feeling the night running away from him*) Where you can't hear
   yourself think?
Gill I mean it's early days, so ...
Sally And you're in the next cabin as well? I can't bear it!
Gill I know, we'll try and behave!

A beat

Mark So what does he do, then ... ?
Gill Oph, all sorts.
Mark Oh right!
Gill He's very different to my usual, you know ...
Sally Great!
Mark What has he ... Does he — work or ... ?
Gill He's been a roadie, he reckons he had a band once but ...
Mark Oh wow!

A beat

Gill And he says he's done films.
Mark Oh, wow?
Gill In Amsterdam, though?
Sally Oh, right!
Gill I know, I daren't ask him too much!

He's — erm ——
Sally What?
Gill — an amazing bloke!
Mark Sounds it!

A beat

Gill He's an amazing bloke!
Sally (*very excited*) I can't believe it!

A beat

Gill I hope you'll like him.
Sally Sounds like you do!
Gill I am a different person, I am, honest! I'll go and get him and we'll
meet you down there, shall I? (*She stands and sways a little*) Oh shit,
it's getting rough now mate, isn't it? It's starting to get rough now!

The three of them sway and grab their drinks

Gill makes her way off stage

The Lights fade to Black-out

Music plays

SCENE 4

Sky Lounge

*The Lights come up on the Sky Lounge setting. The music fades under
the following dialogue*

*Mark turns to the audience, and sits with Sally. They continue their
narration*

Mark (*to the audience*) I couldn't believe it! It was my birthday and
Gill had brought her own little present!
Sally (*to Mark*) We were happy for her, though, weren't we?
Mark (*to the audience*) I wasn't!
Sally (*to the audience*) I told you, he thought he was on for a special.
Mark Well, it wasn't the company I'd expected!

Sally Mind you it was the worst crossing we'd ever been on!

Mark Three Geordies fell overboard and their party didn't notice they were gone until they were on their way back two days later, they were that pissed up.

Sally He's joking.

Mark I'm not!

Sally But if you did fall off what chance have you got?

Mark I wish I'd've fell off to be honest.

Sally He doesn't!

Mark I should have thrown myself off instead of going down to that disco!

Sally It was full of men in their forties with shaven heads!

Mark What's that all about and all? I mean whatever happened to the comb-over?

Mark exits

Sally He'd been trying to get a signal to call his mother and check on the girls. I was sat outside the Irish Bar and the music from the disco was deafening! He'd gone to get another couple of drinks, and the ship wasn't the only thing that was rocking!

Music plays

SCENE 5

Irish Bar

The Lights cross-fade to the Irish Bar and the music fades

Mark enters with a cocktail for Sally. He rejoins her, and presents her with the drink

Mark Be careful with these, they're lethal!

Sally I'm OK!

Mark I know, but it's your third and you usually don't drink!

Sally sips her drink

Sally Did you get through?

Mark I spoke to my dad. I've only got three bars of battery left, so I
didn't stop on! My mam's a bit fluey, he says!
Gill Well, it's that time of year!

Mark sits

Mark So where's Gill?
Sally Probably having a bonk!
Mark Get it out of the way so they don't keep us awake!

Gill enters US. *She looks more fetching than previously, and slightly
raunchy. She is in good spirits*

Gill Oh you're here then? (*She approaches the table*)

Sally watches Gill as she approaches

Sally I was right!
Mark Bull's eye!
Gill It's not bad in here, is it?
Mark (*shouting*) You what?
Gill (*louder*) I said it's not bad ——
Mark You what?
Gill Funny!
Sally (*to Gill*) Everything all right?
Gill Karl's just coming!
Sally Good.
Gill He's had a skinful already by the looks of it!
Mark That's good then!
Gill He's been playing cards with some lorry drivers.
Sally I thought he'd crashed out?
Gill Oh you never know where you are with him, honest!

*Karl enters. He is man in his late forties who looks distinctly
frightening. He drips with gold, which is an odd mix on an older man,
has a number of visible tattoos and a distinctive ear-ring. He has the
mad gaze of a man permanently high on drugs or constantly alerted
to trouble*

*Karl grabs Gill provocatively from behind and mimes a sexual act with
her*

Karl Oi! Oh, what about that? Very nice!

Gill This is Karl! Sally! Mark!
Karl All right?

A moment's tension. Gill feels Karl from behind. Mark stands and shake Karl's hand

Mark Karl?
Karl Not bad!
Sally Nice to meet you!
Mark Can I get you a drink?
Karl I'm all right at the minute, I'm sweating like hell! It's pissing out of me! Boiling in our cabin!
Sally They are warm, we can't get the temperature right in ours!
Karl I'm shagged to be rate!
Sally Oh dear!

Karl sits on the arm of a chair. He is loud and holds court with a commanding air

Karl So then? What we got here? A millionaire then, aren't you?
Mark Sorry?
Karl A millionaire?
Mark Well, not ...
Karl That's what she says! I says, no wonder he can fucking pay for your tickets then! Unless he's after sommat ! (*He laughs and squeezes Gill*) And it's worth every penny!
Gill What is he like, honestly — bloody crackers!
Mark Well, I can probably just about run to a round!

Karl eyes up Sally and Gill

Karl So you two met at college, then?
Sally That's right.
Karl Lesbians then or sommat, were you?

Mark looks stoical

Sally (*happy to bat this back to Karl*) Next best thing, weren't we?
Gill (*mockingly*) Oh definite!
Karl Hey, don't knock it, I like to watch don't you, Mark?
Mark When I get the chance! (*He laughs*)

Karl doesn't find this amusing

Karl I wa' gunna come for some trough but it's full of twats up in that restaurant! And you've got to be dead to want to sit in the Sky Lounge, don't you think?

Mark That's right!

Karl You don't mind me coming, do you? Gill said it'd be all right, but I said I don't fuckin' know you, do I? Don't know if I'm gunna get on wi' you!

Mark Whatever!

Karl He's only saying that! He fucking hates it, really!

Mark It's not a problem!

Karl I says to Gill: be good, coz I know my way around the Dam!

Sally Gill said you'd worked there?

Karl Oh, ay!

Sally Oh, right!

Gill He's done all sorts, haven't you?

Karl Oh, ay, I worked in a sex show for about two month ...

Sally Oh, a sex shop?

Karl *Show* — a sex *show*. I wouldn't work in a sex shop — boring!

Sally Oh, right!

A beat

Karl Mind you, that was boring after a bit ... Just a job isn't it, Mark?

There is an awkward silence

Gill And he was in a band, weren't you?

Sally Really?

Gill And he's roadied, haven't you?

Karl What is it you do Mark, write music for films or sommat?

Mark That's about it.

Karl Loaded, Gill said, you lucky twat!

Mark Hard work, mate.

Karl Fuck off, hard work — what's he like, he expects me to believe that! Is that all tha's done all thee life?

Sally He taught music, didn't you?

Mark My dad was a miner!

Karl Am I supposed to be impressed?

Mark Please yourself!

Karl And what about you, Sally? You just fanny about the village doing nowt, Gill said! Don't have to work!

Gill I never! What is he like honestly?

Karl (*squeezing Gill once more*) I'm only joking! Right are we doing the quiz then or what?

Mark I thought I might pop up to the Sky Lounge, make a few phone calls and I'd like to read for a bit.

Karl It's shit up there, we'll stay in here; we can have a go on the casino later. Lose you some money, bud!

As if the ship swells and dips under the sea's power, the four of them rock and sway, and then become still once more

Oh, here we go, they said it was going to get bad!

Mark They're not wrong.

Karl Do this crossing a lot then?

Mark I used to but I stopped because I couldn't sleep.

Karl I can sleep anywhere!

Mark I think it's my age!

Karl Fifty, aren't you?

Mark Tomorrow!

Karl Nice little surprise then?

Mark Not much!

Karl I'm forty-eight and I can still bench press eighteen stone!

Mark Really?

Karl What's tha weigh, thirteen stone?

Mark Well, about ... !

Karl I could get thee and throw thee off the boat — what about that?

Gill Don't do it on his birthday though, Karl!

Karl Throw thee and a piano off after thee! Tha could play at sea, that'd be a laugh, wouldn't it?

Mark Hilarious!

Karl No, I'll not throw thee off toneet. I'll do it on the way back. Only joking, mate!

Sally He's got an exercise bike haven't you? (*She has a sip of her drink*) Never uses it, but he's got one!

Gill Shall we go and see a film then or what?

Mark (*keen on a change of location*) Yes, that's a good idea!

Karl I'm not watching a fucking film!

Gill Well, why don't you stay here with Mark, then.

Mark No, I'll come with you!

Gill You two stay here and me Sal'l go! Do you fancy a film, Sal?

Sally I'd better do something. I don't want much more to drink or I'll be all over the place!

Karl (*laughing knowingly*) And then you'll be all right, Mark!

Mark That's right!

Gill stands, swaying as if the boat is swaying. Sally joins her. She is a little awkward on her feet

Gill We'll go and have a look at what's on. Are you two going to be all right here?

Karl Ay, and when you come back we'll have a go on the karaoke!

Sally Are you OK with that, Mark?

Karl Ay, he's rate wi' that, aren't you?

A beat

Mark Fine, that's fine!

Gill and Sally head for the exit us. *The four of them sway and rock as the girls make their way*

Sally Am I drunk or is it getting worse?

Mark Both.

The girls giggle their way off

Karl Gill'll be telling t' tale. Telling her all about me!

Mark That's right!

Silence. The two men eye each other uneasily

Karl So do you want another drink, then?

Mark Oh, yes, that'll be nice.

Karl S'tha want?

Mark I'll have a small bottle of red wine if you don't mind!

Karl Hey?

Mark They do a small red wine?

A beat

Karl I'm not ordering that!

Mark Eh?

Karl I'm not ordering wine.

Mark Why not?

Karl Well, it's a twat's drink!

A beat

Mark Well, I'll get it myself then.

A beat

Karl What you saying?

Mark I'm saying I'll get it myself.

Karl You saying I can't afford it?

Mark No, I'm saying I'll get it myself.

Karl I'm not ordering wine on here, they know me. I'll get thee a pint, what's tha want?

Mark I want a small bottle of Jacob's Creek. It's all I drink. I've got high cholesterol.

Karl Tha' trying to be funny? Coz tha's not making much of a job of it.

Mark No!

Karl Tha' could have fooled me.

Mark Well, obviously I have.

Karl (*frustratedly*) Oooh! I can see we're not going to get on, Mark!

Mark Really?

Karl And that's not going to be good, is it?

Mark Isn't it?

Karl Because we've got all weekend together, haven't we? And we don't want to spoil thee birthday, do we?

Mark Not if we can help it!

Karl So then!

A beat

Mark Look, I'll buy my own drink if you've got a problem!

Karl I haven't got a problem; you've got the problem!

A beat

Mark Listen, I don't want a drink!

The two men bounce and sway as if the boat rocks once more

Karl Oooh! That's a good 'un!

Mark Forget it!

Karl looks at Mark in silence. He sits slowly in a chair opposite him

Karl I'll not have one either then.

Mark Whatever!

Silence

Karl So how long have you known Gill, then?

Mark Thirty years!
Karl Right!
Mark Thirty years now!

A beat

Karl You ever shagged her?
Mark Eh?
Karl Have you shagged her?
Mark Wow ... ?
Karl Have you?
Mark No!
Karl But you'd like to?
Mark Hey?
Karl Beat you there then!
Mark Listen ...

A beat

Karl Not that I could do owt about it if you had, like, but I like to know
     where I stand!
Mark Hey, listen....
Karl I bet you've snogged her though, Christmas party or sommat?

A beat

Mark Once!
Karl Once in thirty years? What you playing at?
Mark I've been married twenty-five years pal!
Karl I'm not your pal!
Mark Fine!

A beat

Karl She's mustard though, isn't she?
Mark Well she's a mate, so ... !

A beat

Karl Mind you, these educated women, set of mucky fuckers, aren't
     they?

A beat

Mark Are they?

A beat

Karl I'm straight to the point, me, Mark, I don't mess about. Life's too
   short.
Mark It is, you're right!

Silence

Karl And let me give you a word of advice. Don't stare!
Mark What?
Karl Don't stare at me.

A beat

Mark I wasn't staring at you.
Karl Yes, you were!
Mark I wasn't!
Karl Liar!
Mark I wasn't staring at you!

A beat

Karl What you got a funny eye then or what?
Mark I wasn't staring at you!

A beat

Karl I've been about a bit, Mark!
Mark So have I.
Karl Have you?
Mark I have!
Karl What, playing the piano?
Mark Listen, mate I think we've ...

A beat

Karl I know what you're thinking, mate.
Mark What am I thinking then?

A beat

Karl You're thinking I'm a twat!
Mark You're not wrong there!

Karl You're thinking what's Gill doing with this twat?

A beat

Mark Hey, listen …
Karl I like her, man!
Mark Whatever!
Karl I like her!
Mark So do I!
Karl I know that, she's told me! She's told me all about you!

The tension relaxes

   Do you smoke?
Mark No.
Karl Don't mind if I ... ?
Mark If you have to.
Karl I don't have to, mate, but I want to.

Karl takes a moment, looks around and lights a cigarette. He deliberately blows smoke in Mark's face

   You like Springsteen, then? Seen him before?
Mark No. Have you?
Karl Twice!
Mark Really?
Karl No, I'm fucking you about! (*He thinks this is hilarious*)
Mark That's good then!

A beat

Karl I'm not a twat, mate!
Mark No?

A beat

Karl We used to earn some money touring. Big bands, man! Seventies
   bands, Uriah Heep! The Groundhogs! Floyd!
Mark Yes?
Karl Family!
Mark Good band!

A beat

Karl And the fanny man!
Mark Yes ...
Karl 'Kin'ell!
Mark Yes?

A beat

Karl Mind you — Gill!
Mark Yeh?

A beat

Karl I don't think she's had owt for ages!
Mark There you go!

A beat

Karl But tha's happily married, isn't tha?
Mark Well, I wouldn't go that far.

A beat

Karl Kids though, I don't fancy that fucking lark! Has she got her eye
    on it, does tha' know?
Mark I've no idea. mate!

Karl finishes smoking

Karl No, I don't fancy that!

A beat

Mark She's a good mate!
Karl Meaning what?
Mark She deserves a break!

A beat

Karl She's getting one.
Mark That's right!
Karl That is right!

A beat

Mark Good!
Karl That is good!

A beat

> Now I'm getting thee a pint whether tha' likes it or not! Coz I'm not
> a twat!
Mark That's right, you're not a twat!

Mark and Karl sway together as if the boat is rocking

Mark ⎫ *(together)* Ooow!
Karl ⎭

> *Karl makes his way* US *and exits*

Mark returns to the Sky Lounge setting and sits

The Lights fade to Black-out

Music changes

SCENE 6

Sky Lounge

*The Lights come up; a spotlight gently picks Mark up but the rest of the
stage is visible*

The music fades and plays quietly under the following scene

Mark *(to the audience)* About an hour later Gill and Sally had come
back from the cinema. Sally had been sick twice, but insisted on
having a port and a packet of peanuts. Well, that was a mistake. I think
she was looking for a way out — she wasn't by herself!

> *Sally enters with a drink and sits at the table*

Sally *(to the audience)* You see I don't usually drink, I must have been
carried away by all the excitement!
Mark Where did she say she found him anyway?

Sally In prison, she said. She'd done some storytelling workshops in a day prison and they hit it off! She told me he's the best lover she'd ever had!

Mark Which I find a bit depressing, if I'm honest!

Sally Told you he was jealous!

Mark Anyway by last orders I'd had about five pints which Karl had forced down me!

Sally And we found ourselves down in the disco, smiling like we'd gone mad, while he did the karaoke for us!

Mark Which was good of him!

Sally My face was aching I was smiling that much!

Mark And at half one he insisted that we had the last dance — together!

Sally There was only us and the ship's policeman still standing!

The Lights fade to Black-out

Music plays: Neil Diamond singing "You Don't Bring Me Flowers"

SCENE 7

Disco

The Lights come up

Mark and Sally are still seated. The table is crowded with empty glasses

Gill enters. She looks very drunk and bedraggled, and is carrying drinks. Karl enters with a number of drinks. He too is the worse for wear

The four of them bob and sway as if the ship has hit a big wave

Karl (*screaming his head off at Mark*) Argh! Argh! Hey it's been brilliant, hasn't it?

Mark That's right!

Karl I said it would be! Right I love this! Come on, come on Sally, up naa!

Sally I don't think I can!

Karl Up naa! Up naaa!

Karl manhandles Sally from her seat; she struggles to stand

Come on here! You bugger! Naa! This is nice.
Sally Oh hell!

Karl smooches with Sally

Karl (*to Mark*) Thee dance with Gill.
Mark Oh, no, mate!
Karl Tha's snogged her, hasn't tha? A dance wain't hurt.
Mark No I'm right!
Karl Thee dance with fucking Gill! Tha knows tha fancies her, what tha
   playing at? Up naa!

*Karl dances with Sally. Both of them are tired and a little shy. Mark and
Gill dance close*

Karl (*singing*) You don't bring me flowers any more! (*Speaking*) Lovely
   this, it's lovely, Sally. Do you like it?
Sally I do, it's lovely.
Karl It is lovely!
Sally It is lovely!
Karl I love Neil Diamond; it's wank but I love it!

The couples sway around the stage

Mark and Gill come into focus. There is still a strong spark here!

Mark We've got to dance then.
Gill Don't!
Mark What?
Gill Make fun!
Mark Thanks for my present! When does he have to go back?
Gill Where to?
Mark The nut house!

A beat

Gill Are you mad at me?
Mark I can't be, can I?
Gill Thanks.
Mark You look great.
Gill Kiss me!

Mark kisses Gill

Mark Oh Gill!
Gill He's a lovely bloke!
Mark Yes?
Gill He's a lovely bloke!

Karl leaves Sally and comes to Mark and Gill

Karl Right. Bed time! Come on, let's get you sorted. Night you two, see you tomorrow: when we will see the Boss! And don't keep us awake shagging!

Karl sings as he sways upstage with Gill. Both sway and roll

Oh Thunder Road!

Karl and Gill exit

SCENE 8

Sky Lounge

The Lights cross-fade to the Sky Lounge

The Neil Diamond song is replaced by piano music seeping in under the dialogue

Mark and Sally move back to the Sky Lounge

Mark (*to the audience*) And then they just floated out of the disco.
Sally (*to the audience*) And down the corridors, rocking from side to side!
Mark The ship was all over the place!
Sally It was that bad they'd told you not to go out on deck!
Mark (*looking at the mess on the table*) I'll take some of these back, do you want another?
Sally Not for me.

Mark collects some of the glasses and exits

It was gone two o'clock when we got back to our cabin. It was boiling, and I felt awful. I mean, like I've said, I don't usually drink, but what with it being Mark's birthday, and seeing Gill and meeting Boris Karloff — that's what he'd christened him ... I told him, if he had ever found out, he would have thrown him off the boat.

*Mark enters with a large truck of a cabin door frame which he fixes c.
He sets up the cabin setting during the following, with a chair*

Mark I wasn't bothered. I went crackers when we got in the cabin! I
said we were never going on holiday with anybody else ever again.
Sally Not even the kids!
Mark There was water driving onto the side of the window. It was rain,
but I told her it was the water line.
Sally I wasn't bothered, I just wanted to die.
Mark I didn't feel good myself, but she'd been sick twice.
Sally I couldn't help it, honestly!
Mark There were peanuts all over the floor! And she was just sat there
like death warmed up!

There is the sound of a howling wind

SCENE 9

Cabin

The Lights tighten in focus to give the impression of a small cabin

Sally moves and sits on the chair in the cabin. She is desperately ill

Mark stands near her. He too is slightly drunk

Mark Feel any better?
Sally Not really!
Mark Are you going to be sick again?
Sally How do I know?
Mark Well if you don't, who does?

A beat

Sally What's that?
Mark What?
Sally That banging?

Silence

Mark That's the ship sinking, darling!
Sally Don't be …
Mark Sounds like some chains catching.

They rock a little more

Sally Time is it?
Mark Ten to three, only another four hours, and they'll let us off!
Sally I'll be dead! I wish we'd gone by plane.
Mark So do I and I hate flying.

A beat

Sally Urgh, I feel off it!
Mark Lie down.
Sally Can't you hear that?
Mark It's the anchor, isn't it?
Sally Not that, that?
Mark What?
Sally Somebody's shouting. (*She listens carefully*) Can't you hear that?
   (*She listens again*)

Mark listens too

   It's him and Gill!
Mark Oh, hell, where are my headphones?
Sally You didn't bring them.
Mark Bloody hell!
Sally Oh, I feel awful!
Mark Well, what're you listening for then?

Mark and Sally rock and roll with the boat once more

Sally I can hear him, but I can't hear Gill any more.
Mark Maybe he's eaten her?

Silence

Sally I think she's eating him.
Mark Oh, I'm going outside!
Sally What for?
Mark I can't listen to that, not today! I want to get some fresh air. I feel
   a bit sick.

Sally Well, go in the sink.

Mark I can't, it's full of peanuts!

Sally I don't want to be worrying about where you are!

Mark I'll just go see if my dad's rung back!

Sally (*angrily*) We're in the middle of the sea — give your parents a miss.

Mark Except they've been ill every time I've been away. I just want to check! I couldn't get a signal in the disco!

Sally God help me!

Mark I know it's not sexy having ailing parents, I'm sorry!

Sally Why are you starting this now?

Mark I can't believe you're bringing this up!

Sally Why are you shouting?

Mark Why are you?

Sally Because you never give to this family; you're still living at home, even though you've got kids! You're never there for me when I need you!

Mark You feel sick for God's sake, that's all!

Sally It's not about that and you know it's not!

Mark No that's right!

Sally (*angrily*) You've got a piece of music you can't finish and it's sending you round the bend. Leave it, pack it in, get a proper job! Get out of your head and join the real world!

Mark I've seen the real world, and it's a bit scary actually! It's next door shagging our Carla's godmother unless you'd forgotten!

Banging is heard from next door

Sally Stop shouting; they're banging at us!

Mark Yes, he probably wants us both in there! Well you can please yourself!

Sally What are you going to do out there?

Mark Throw myself off the bastard thing!

Sally Mark! Urph! (*She retches at Mark*)

Mark Oph these are new shoes!

Mark storms US *and out of the cabin, as he does he spins the door frame and is transported to the exterior at the back of the boat*

SCENE 10

The Deck

The Lights change to indicate a bad storm; the festoon lights shake even more. The sound of a howling wind comes up and then fades. We get the sense that there is a terribly cold wind and a dreadfully antagonistic sea!

Mark moves DS

Sally stands

Sally I must have fallen asleep, didn't wake up till the next morning, when I discovered I was wrapped in toilet paper and covered in peanuts; so goodness knows where I slept!

Sally exits

Mark (*shouting above the soundscape*) I stayed out on deck. I was trying to get a signal on my phone. I had one bar left on my battery, it was just enough to check for my messages. (*He fiddles with his phone*)

Karl enters. During the following he rolls what must only be a joint

Both men speak over the wind

Karl Argh, he's here! All right?

A beat

Heard you arguing!
Mark It comes to us all!

A beat

Karl Gill, can't get enough of it.
Mark That's good then!
Karl I stink of her!
Mark Lovely!

Karl lights the joint

Karl Do you want a blast?
Mark I don't do dope!
Karl What do you do?
Mark Red wine!

Karl smokes his joint. He adjusts his crotch

Karl My knob!
Mark (*trying to get a message*) I've got a message here!

Karl draws on his joint; he has the giggles. Mark accesses his message

Karl So we'll come with you in the car tomorra! What you got?
Mark A new Renault.
Karl Listen to him, a new Renault? Well, we'll check in the hotel and then I'll show you the way to see the city.

Mark angles the phone to hear his message. He can hardly hear it

Mark Oh for fu … !
Karl You got a message?

Mark is visibly shaken

   Karl prepares to exit

Mark Yes, my mother again; another heart job!

Karl giggles

Karl Oph, how old is she then, man?
Mark She's eighty-two now!
Karl And she going for another job?
Mark It's a heart job mate!
Karl Well she must fucking like it man!
Mark Like what?
Karl Art!
Mark That's right!

A beat

Karl We'll do Van Gogh and all, oph my knob's killing me!
Mark (*dead*) Is it?

Karl turns to depart

Karl Listen, you and your lady, and me and my lady, we're going to
have a weekend we'll never forget, aren't we?
Mark We are!
Karl We fucking are and all! I'll show you the sights, man, I'll show
you the sights! (*He tries to move us, struggling. Suddenly turning*)
Hey, if you want to have a go at me do it now, because you'll never
have another chance all right! (*To himself*) You'll never have another
chance!

Karl exits through the door to the boat, after a struggle

Mark watches him and then looks out to the audience

Mark (*to the audience*) I should have pushed him off the boat; I don't
know why I didn't. And I wanted to laugh at him! But there was
something about him that wasn't funny! And let's be honest I know
how men like him have been let down, not developed, ignored! But
mostly at that moment I thought he was a fucking pig! But he had
liberated something in me — and I wasn't sure what it was until we
got to Amsterdam. No it wasn't until we got to Amsterdam.

Music plays: "Tomorrow Night" by Atomic Rooster

The Lights fade slowly

*Mark goes to seek some shelter up by the door frame C and tries to get
a signal on his phone*

Black-out

ACT II

SCENE 1

Rotterdam

The Lights are up on a pre-set: an open, empty space, the table and chairs which signified the boat in Act I having been struck. Music plays

The lighting pre-set fades; the music fades

Sally enters

The Lights come up

Sally (*directly to the audience*) One of the things about getting the car on the boat last, is that you can often get it off first. Which is great, if you want to get straight on the road! It was just our luck, wasn't it? Because of the storm, some water had got into the engine and it wouldn't start, so Mark had to push it off!

Mark enters pushing a small car (but big enough to hold four people); he positions it c as he narrates the story

Mark (*to the audience*) I pushed it to the top of the ramp and it started as we rolled down.
Sally We'd arrived in Rotterdam in a heavy sea fret!
Mark So we could have been anywhere!
Sally And then we had to wait for Boris and Gill. Who were dead to the world. He thought somebody had thrown him off!
Mark Yes, but nothing goes the way I want it.
Sally They reckon you've to be careful what you wish for!
Mark I know what I'd wished for. A big whale to come up and eat him.
Sally I think he'd wished for something else to be honest.
Mark I couldn't get over the cheek; two hundred quid return trip tickets for the concert, the hotel and Gill had brought Frankenstein!

Sally gets into the car. She ruffles her hair so she looks rough and as if she feels awful

Sally So we waited in the car for about an hour, didn't we? I felt awful and I looked like I'd spent a night in a toilet!
Mark Which she had!
Sally I mean it was insane.
Mark We'd been waiting for that long, the port authorities thought we were on a stake-out.

Mark gets into the car, and the atmosphere changes immediately. The Lights tighten to light just the car. Low smoke blows in to give the impression of a haze of morning mist. We hear the horn of a ship and the ripple of water

Sally Oph!
Mark Rough?
Sally Oph!

Mark rubs his face; he is exhausted

   Did you sleep?
Mark Not really.

A beat

Sally How long did you stay outside for?
Mark Too long.
Sally That's just ... !
Mark I saw England disappear then I came in.
Sally Weren't you cold?
Mark Well, I couldn't feel my hands! That's why I left you on the toilet floor.
Sally Thanks for that!
Mark Well, you were asleep!
Sally In a pool of peanuts.
Mark You looked cosy.

A beat

Sally So what did Boris do then?
Mark Had a joint and disappeared; I think he went looking for some cheesecake. I told him about my mum and he just started laughing. Off his head! He was nearly over the side then; never mind what he can bench press. (*Beat*) And he only said that to threaten me!
Sally No he didn't, you're paranoid!

Mark He's a predator! He was putting down his scent!

A beat

Sally Well,why didn't you put down yours?

A beat

Mark I haven't got much left, I want to save some of it! (*Beat*) I should
have pushed him over the side: he wouldn't have been laughing then!
I'd liked to have seen him munch his way out of that!

Sally looks at her watch. They are becoming uncomfortable

Sally An hour now, this is bloody barmy!
Mark Well, we can go if you want!
Sally We can't!
Mark We can, nothing would give me more pleasure!
Sally We can't just leave 'em on the boat, can we?
Mark Why can't we? What's stopping us?
Sally You don't do it though, do you?
Mark Why don't you?
Sally Well, it's bad manners!
Mark I will happily drive off now, just give the word.

A beat

Sally Oh, we can't, can we?
Mark Yes, we can, but we must go now or we'll be trapped.
Sally Don't be like that
Mark We'll be trapped, Sal, and they might try and eat us!

A beat

Sally Oh, it's not that bad, is it?
Mark This is what they ought to do with them celebrities. Never mind
the Bushtucker Trials; let them have two nights on a North Sea ferry
with a psychopath and see who wants to go home!
Sally He's not a psycho, is he?
Mark He's as near as you get! He said he'll show us the best way to
see the city!
Sally What did he mean?
Mark I've got no idea! (*He impersonates a stoned Karl*) "You and your
lady and me and my lady."

Sally Oh right!
Mark I thought he was going to burst into song!
Sally Well, if he's worked there ...

A beat

Mark Well I'm not going to any dodgy clubs. You can go, but I'm not; there is no way I'm going to watch some nubile law student play about with a bodybuilder — it's depressing.
Sally Why is it?
Mark Because it is!

A beat

Sally Is it because you're with me?

A beat

Mark Meaning what?
Sally It's because you're with me, isn't it?
Mark Why is it?

A beat

Sally I bet you've been to them on your own?
Mark What makes you say that?
Sally Because I know you!
Mark What do you mean?

A beat

Sally Well, we used to find things like that exciting!
Mark Things like what?
Sally Well, you had them books, didn't you?
Mark It was twenty years ago!
Sally It's only the same!

A beat

Mark I thought you felt off it?
Sally Well, I don't feel good!
Mark Well, give it a miss then!

A beat

Sally I mean that's why most people go to Amsterdam, they're going to go and have a look. I don't know what they expect if they get in there. I don't know how different it's going to be.

Mark It's just more straightforward, I imagine! It's like going into a sweet shop! Down by the "Pick 'n' Mix". I'll have one of them and one of them! How much? Smashing!

Sally I suppose he'll want to show off to Gill.

Mark He's been showing off to Gill all night if you ask me!

Sally Well, anyway!

Mark Well, I'm not going in any dodgy clubs! And I'm not getting stoned either!

A beat

Sally You were stoned at college, though, weren't you?

Mark Meaning what?

Sally In fact you were stoned more than anybody else; you overdid everything!

Mark Well, yes, but ... !

Sally I mean there were seven women to every bloke — and you were like a dog with two tails!

A beat

Mark Why are you bringing this up?

Sally I'm only saying ——

Mark It's my birthday and —— !

Sally I know but let's be fair; you wanted to shag everything that moved didn't you? If it moved shag it, if it didn't put it in your Foundation Course file, you used to say!

Mark Well, anyway —— !

Sally I mean you were the Karl of the College weren't you?

Mark Well, anyway —— !

Sally That's why he's got to you!

Mark Well, anyway —— !

A beat

Sally I mean I knew all about you! I even knew about you and Katie Shannon.

A beat

Mark How did you know that, then?

Sally Gill told me.

A beat

Mark Good old Gill.

A beat

Sally And I know that you tried to bed her when I was bad that New Year with shingles.

A beat

Mark She told you that and all, did she?
Sally It was at Mike Johnson's party in Headingley.
Mark Bloody Gill!
Sally She used to tell me everything.
Mark Well, if she tells you about last night, keep it to yourself — I don't want to know!

A beat

Sally So what did your dad say when you spoke to him?
Mark They were still in A and E, been there six hours. Shortage of doctors!
Sally (*beginning to feel queasy*) I feel like the car's moving.
Mark Well, it's not!
Sally Feel like I'm still on the boat.
Mark Tony Blair didn't have to wait when his heart went out of rhythm, did he?
Sally I feel like the road's moving!
Mark Mind you if I have many more nights like last night my heart'll be out of rhythm. Feel like I've got Ronnie Scott in my chest.
Sally (*getting uneasy*) Where the bloody hell are they?
Mark Well they weren't up at eight o'clock. Mind you, when that breakfast call went off I was fast asleep. I thought the ship was going down. (*He does the ship's announcement*) Bing Bong! It's six o'clock! Get up! Breakfast is now being served on D deck, if you're sober enough to keep anything down.
Sally Oh, don't!

A beat

Mark You know, we hardly know Gill, really, do we?

Sally Course we do!

Mark We don't.

Sally Well, you've tried to get to know her!

Mark I mean she's a godmother but we don't know her — didn't she
have to take an oath or something?

Sally Yes, but it didn't say anything about her choice of bed partners!

A beat

Mark It'll not last, you know!

Sally Well, if she's happy.

Mark I mean what's she trying to do, save him?

Sally Well, she didn't want to save you, did she?

Mark No, she didn't!

Sally She was happy to let you drown. Ogh, I feel rough! (*She reacts to
a wave of nausea*)

Mark Here! (*He hands her a sick bag*)

Sally Thanks.

Mark I've got a load.

Sally (*looking daggers at Mark*) What?

Mark Nothing.

Sally Well, don't look at me like that.

Mark Hey, don't you start, I had enough last night with nutty saying I
was staring at him!

A beat

Sally We've got to give them a chance, they're in love!

Mark Oh, come on!

Sally What?

Mark Oh!

Sally They are!

Mark Do you believe that?

Sally Well, I know it's early days, but …

Mark If you really believe that …

Sally Look, I feel rough, OK, let's not make everything an argument!

A beat

Mark He's only after one thing!

Sally Well, he's a bloke isn't he — surprise, surprise!

Mark Yes, I know. He was the bloke who made my life a misery at
school.

Sally What, him?

Mark Kids like him. When I was learning the piano they'd stand on the wall outside Mrs Pearson's and wave their knob at me.

Sally You never told me that!

Mark Well it's not the sort of thing you want to share is it? Mrs Pearson never saw them; she only had one good eye and that was on the sheet music! It's a wonder I ever learned to play when I think about it! And when I was going home they'd piss on me from the top of the bus stop. I mean nobody learned the piano on our estate in nineteen-sixty-four; it was the equivalent of wearing a dress in public! They've always had it in for me!

Sally You're paranoid!

Mark I know men, I've been one for fifty years! They're nasty bastards!

A beat

Sally Well, Gill must think he's got something!

Mark Well, she's desperate, isn't she?

Sally Well, I wouldn't — —

Mark How old is she? She's younger than us! I mean we both had a year in the real world, Gill went straight from a convent school, didn't she?

Sally Can't remember.

Mark It was like giving gin to the Indians when she came to college! And now she's at the last chance saloon! Her whole life's been like a western.

A beat

Sally Well, if she likes him ...?

Mark Oh, man!

Sally He's making her feel good.

A beat

Mark Meaning what?

Sally He's making her feel good about herself.

Mark Meaning what?

Sally What?

Mark What?

A beat

Sally Well, you do spend a lot of time in the spare room.
Mark When I'm working.
Sally I'm only saying.
Mark What are you saying?
Sally You spend a lot of time in the spare room.

A beat

Mark Well, I mean if you made the same sort of effort ...

A beat

Sally Eh?
Mark Well.
Sally What?
Mark It's like you always say, Gill dresses provocatively.
Sally Cheap!
Mark Well!

A beat

Sally So I don't dress right?

A beat

Mark I thought you didn't feel well?

A beat

Sally So I don't dress right, what do you want me to do, dress like a fruit stall?
Mark I can't talk to you!
Sally What do you want me to do?
Mark Oh leave it!

A beat

Sally I mean she's said he makes her feel about sixteen so she should be wearing a school uniform.
Mark She probably does!
Sally Is that what you want me to do?

A beat

Mark I think they're doing the stuff you do when you're sixteen, to be honest.

Sally Well, don't begrudge her that.

A beat

Mark Sounds like you're jealous.

Sally Well, I know you are! I saw your face drop!

A beat

Mark So you'd like to feel what she's feeling?

Sally Don't be daft.

Mark Admit it.

Sally What?

Mark You'd like to feel sixteen again.

Sally No, I wouldn't.

A beat

Mark Well, I bloody would.

Sally Well, there you go, then, you know what to do.

A beat

Mark I'll let him shove his fingers up my arse, then shall I?

Sally I thought you didn't like him?

A beat

Mark I'll end up having a heart attack, never mind my Mother. Supposed to be a birthday treat and I'm stuck with a nymphomaniac and a mad bastard! I bet he's got six ton of resin stuck up his backend and all. If we get stopped with any dope in this car, I will go frigging barmy.

Sally Oh, stop going on, please!

Mark I'm serious, if he gets any dope out in this car I will hit the roof!

Black-out

Music plays: "Radar Love"

The Car

The music fades and plays under the following scene as if coming from a car radio

The Lights come up focussing on the car with an effect that gives the impression of movement

Gill and Karl have joined Sally and Mark in the car; they sit in the back seat. Karl is rolling a joint. Gill is extremely excited and she and Karl are all over each other; they are in the heady haze of being drunk and stoned. By contrast, Mark — who is driving — and Sally are less pleased

Gill Roll another!
Karl I'll roll another!
Gill Roll another!
Karl I'm rolling another!
Gill Excellent!
Karl I'm gunna roll another, babe!
Sally (*to Mark*) Say something!
Mark What?
Sally I thought you were going to say something?
Mark Leave it!
Sally I thought you were going to say something?
Mark You say something!
Sally Why don't you?
Mark What good would it do, they're out of their heads? They don't even know they're off the bloody boat!

Sharp looks pass between Mark and Sally

  Open a window.
Sally Why?
Mark Just open a window!
Sally And then what?
Mark Let's jump out!
Sally They are smoking dope in our car, Mark.
Mark Yes, I know that.
Sally Well, I thought you were going to do something?
Mark What do you want me to do, join in?

Gill (*leaning forward to talk with Sally and Mark*) Hey, sorry about this, mate!
Sally No problem.
Gill I know it's ever so rude …
Sally Well, it is a bit …
Gill Yeah, I'm sorry, Sal, do you want a blast of this? (*She offers a well-toked joint to Sally*)
Sally Not for me, Gill, I'm still a bit ...
Gill What?
Sally I'm still on the boat.
Gill Are you?
Sally You know, moving!
Gill Oph.
Sally I'm still going up and down!
Gill I was going up and down all night!

A beat

Sally Yes, I know that!
Karl (*leaning forward*) This is good stuff, this!
Sally Is it?
Karl It's been treated with horse tranquillizer.
Sally I hope it works, then!
Karl D'you want a blast, Mark?
Mark Not for me, I've had some of that.
Karl Have you?
Mark Years ago, sent me to sleep, mate!
Karl Oh, man!
Mark So smoke as much as you like!

Gill looks slightly confused!

Gill (*to Karl*) Sally say's she's still on the boat!

A beat

Karl No, she's not!
Gill Isn't she?
Karl No, she's sat there!

Karl and Gill think this is hilarious

Gill She's sat there! Oh man!

Karl Man!
Gill Man!
Karl She thinks she's on the boat, but she's in a car ...
Gill Oh, man.
Karl Oh, shit.
Gill She's hallucinating!!
Karl She doesn't know where she is, oh heavy man!

They are in fits of laughter

Mark I'm going to crash the car in a minute.
Sally Good.
Mark Just so you know!
Gill (*coming forward once more*) Hey, can you remember at college?
   We'd get stoned and go sit in the park listening to Grace Slick and all
   we'd eat was Marmite on toast! Can you remember? Is there any toast
   in the car, Mark?
Mark Sorry, Gill, we're right out of toast.

Sally looks uncomfortable

Sally Don't have too much, Gill?
Gill Oh, shit, my mother's turned up!

Gill and Karl laugh loudly

Karl Helps prevent arthritis, you know? My mother was riddled with
   it.
Mark Medicinal then?
Karl Riddled with it. I don't fucking fancy that!
Sally (*attempting a fight back*) I'm sorry if we kept you awake last
   night!
Gill Who?
Sally Coz we were at it, weren't we?
Gill Just like us — I am shagged, honestly!

Mark looks at Sally like she has lost the plot

Sally Sorry if we embarrassed you!
Gill They wouldn't embarrass us, would they?
Sally (*to Mark*) Great, wasn't it?
Mark (*disbelievingly*) Oh, yeah, brilliant!
Gill (*screaming at the top of her voice with joy*) Oh, I love this; it's
   brilliant! Just cruising with mates.
Karl Arghhh!

Gill leans forward once more

Gill Karl said your Mum had gone for a job! How did she get on?
Mark What?
Gill She'd gone for a job?
Mark My mother's in hospital, Gill!
Gill Oh why?
Mark She's had a heart job.
Karl I thought she'd gone for a job?
Mark She's had a heart do!
Karl Oh, man ... (*He laughs again*) I thought it was a fucking art course or sommat!
Gill He said she's gone for an art job, I thought where, you know, at that time? But they have open classes and stuff, so ...
Mark Her heart's out of rhythm!
Karl Well, listen, she's in the best place, mate.
Mark Yes?
Karl Trust me man, she's in the best fucking place!

A beat

Mark Lucky her!

A beat

Karl Mind you, I lost my mother when I was ten. No ties at all me. No family to call owt! (*He realizes he needs another blast on the joint*) Hey, don't Bogart that joint, Gill, man, put me on! Pick me to play man, I've got my kit on!

Gill has a final toke on the joint and gives it to Karl

Gill He's got no family, have you?
Karl (*becoming angry*) Went away when I was twelve. My Dad couldn't do fuck all wi' me, man! I've got a sister,man; she worked for P and O ferries. Made her redundant! Bastards, man, for laying her off. But I tell you what, man!
Mark What?

Karl takes a big toke, and holds it!

Karl Nice boats! (*He breathes out in the front of the car then hitches himself so he can speak closer to Mark*) Hey, listen, you know, I think we might have got off on the wrong footing yesterday.

Mark Don't worry about it!
Karl I'm not!
Mark Good.

Karl takes exception to Mark's gaze

Karl Hey, what have I told you? Don't stare!
Mark Right!
Karl I only warn once! I'm letting you off because I like you!
Mark That's good then!

A beat

Karl Yes, I think we might have got off to a bad start mate.

A beat

Mark Yes. I think you're right. I mean I was going to throw you off the
    boat last night but I decided not to.
Karl Yeah?
Mark Yes!

*Karl suddenly grabs Mark around the neck in a manic act of utter vio-
lence. The car swerves all over*

Karl I'd like to fucking see you try.
Mark Argh!
Karl I'd like to see you!
Mark (*struggling to breathe*) I can't …
Gill Karl?
Sally Watch the road!
Mark (*to Sally*) What do you want me to do?
Sally Watch the road!
Mark (*trying to steer*) I'm watching the bloody road!
Karl (*laughing at his antics*) I'd like to see you!
Sally Watch the road!
Mark I have got Nutty Nut around my neck, by the way!
Sally (*trying to help Mark; to Karl*) Get off him you great silly sod!

Karl insanely attempts to choke Mark

Karl Eh? Eh? I'd like to see you …
Mark I choking …

Karl Eh? Eh? Eh?
Mark I can't breathe, you soft ...
Sally Gill, stop him, Mark's turning blue.
Gill Karl? Put him down, put him down, man!
Mark (*choking*) Put me down, man!
Sally (*screaming*) Put him down!
Gill Down, Karl down!

The car swerves all over the place. Gill fights to free up Mark. Karl lets go, sits back and Mark coughs and splutters

Karl Argh ... ! Feel that power? Strong!
Mark You stupid ...
Karl Stupid? Stupid?
Gill He's only playing with you, Mark.
Karl I'm only playing with you, man ...

Mark adjusts his collar. Karl is now extremely calm and composed

Mark Oh hell ... !
Karl Look at his face. It's what we used to do when I was roadie-ing, man! Tell you what before the gig, I'll take us all out.
Mark Don't bother.

Karl playfully rubs Mark's hair as if Mark is a little boy

Karl Oh, now, he's a got a bear on!
Mark I bloody well have and all!
Karl (*laughing*) I'll take us to a right place! Best place in Amsterdam. Argh, we're going to have a good time.

Sally cares for Mark. Springsteen's "Dancing in the Dark" can be heard playing under, quietly

Sally Are you OK?
Mark (*whispers*) This is insane!
Sally Well, don't look at me like that!
Mark It was your idea to invite Gill because she'd not been anywhere. Well, you were wrong there, weren't you? She's been to bloody hell and back!
Karl Hey, turn this up, I love this! (*He leans forwards and turns up the radio*)

The volume of the music increases. Gill and Karl immediately start to rock along to the song

Mark and Sally get out of the car

The Lights fade to Black-out

   Sally, Gill and Karl exit taking the car with them

SCENE 3

Amsterdam

The Lights come up on Mark and the music fades

Mark, rather worn and shattered, moves DS

Mark (*directly to the audience*) Hey, listen, this is not a story this is my bloody life here! We arrived in Amsterdam about two hours later. Gill and Boris had smoked that much grass that checking into the hotel was hilarious, they couldn't remember their names or nationality.

Sally enters with a bike and picks up the narration

Sally   (*to the audience*) He'd booked us into the hotel Grand Kransnapolsky. Three hundred and twenty quid a night — he didn't tell me that at the time.
Mark Would you have?
Sally And after Karl had ordered room service he wanted to show us the Sex Museum!
Mark Yes, he was marking his place in it!

Mark exits

Sally Then he insisted we hired some bikes; said it was the only way to see the city. And of course if anyone was going to get a dodgy one it was Mark, His chain came off when we followed a canal out of the city, and we lost him for half an hour. The sun had come out and we had a picnic in the shade of some lime trees near the canal! It was almost pleasant actually!

SCENE 4

Canal Picnic

*The Lights change; a gobo gives the effect of light through lime trees.
There are the sounds of birds and barges*

Sally parks her bike US

  Karl and Gill enter with bikes

They park up their bikes, and make a small area C *their own*

Gill Oh, this is lovely here!
Karl Ay, we're rate here!
Gill Will Mark find us, do you think?
Sally Well, if he follows the canal he can't miss us!
Karl This is more like it. Two ladies and a man!
Gill Ay ay ...

*The three of them position themselves on the ground. Gill and Karl are
very sensual with each other. Karl opens a tinfoil-wrapped piece of cake,
and begins to eat it*

Sally All right, then?
Karl Ay, are you?
Sally Not bad.
Gill Good.
Karl That's good, then!

A beat

Karl You ever had three in a bed, Sally?
Sally Sorry?
Karl You ever had three in a bed?

A beat

Sally I've had five in a bed actually.
Karl Oh wow.
Gill Really?

A beat

Sally Three of them were under ten, and they all had chicken pox but
  you know I think it still counts.
Karl Oh, man, she's funny.
Sally I have my moments.

*Karl offers Sally a piece of cake. It is space cake but Sally is not to
know*

Karl You want a piece of this or what?
Sally Do you mind? I'm ravenous. I haven't eaten since we got off the
  boat. I couldn't keep anything down! (*She bites into the cake*)
Karl Is Mark all right then or what?
Sally He's fine.

Karl relaxes with Gill

Karl I love it out here, this is some city.
Sally It's great when you get out of the centre ...

A beat

Karl It's the people though, they're so, what's the word?
Sally Tall!
Karl Chilled!

Karl and Gill all over each other

Gill He's done all sorts out here, haven't you?
Karl Oh, ay, all sorts. Bands, women! I've had three in a bed, and been
  paid for it.
Gill What's he like?

A beat

Sally Don't tell Mark that, he'll hang himself!
Karl He doesn't like me, does he?
Sally What makes you say that?
Karl I tell you sommat, I'm on my fucking best behaviour and all!
Gill He is, aren't you?
Karl I tell you what, princess, what we want here are some beers!
Gill Oh, yes, that'll be cool!
Karl You want a beer Sal, or what? (*He stands*)
Sally Well, I don't usually drink and drive.
Karl Well, tha's having one so knackers!

Karl exits

Silence

Gill All right?
Sally Yes!
Gill Good.
Sally That's good then!

A beat

Gill It's a good gig.
Sally What?
Gill It's a good gig, Sal.
Sally Whatever!

A beat

Gill And it's fun.
Sally Hey, I'm not judging.
Gill I wondered.
Sally No, I'm ——

Silence

Gill So how's everything then?
Sally Do you want the truth or what we tell everybody?
Gill Whatever!
Sally Do you want the "happy wealthy couple with three gorgeous girls" story? Or do you want the "in the spare bed, always bickering, still lives with his parents" story? And then there's the "threats that he's going to leave" story! That a good one! Which one do you want?

A beat

Gill I like the one about everything being OK.
Sally So do I, but I don't believe it!

A beat

Gill Is there anything you can do?
Sally You mean apart from walk off a cliff?

A beat

Gill What about your sex life?
Sally Oh, come on, what sex life?
Gill Well.

A beat

Sally We heard, by the way; the whole roasted hog! We heard you!
Gill Sorry, mate!
Sally That's why Mark went on deck. You know he's got this thing about you, always has?
Gill What is he like, honestly?
Sally I sometimes think you and him would have made the better couple.
Gill Ohh!
Sally I'm serious!

A beat

Gill Well all this is complete eye-opener!
Sally I know and I'm jealous. That's the truth. I pretend I'm not, but I am.
Gill Jealous of me?
Sally Oh come on, you know it!
Gill I've always been jealous of you — the house, the kids! You wouldn't want to change all that, would you? That's so weird, now!
Sally Probably not!
Gill That's the risk!

A beat

Sally So are you trying to save him, or what?
Gill From what?
Sally From himself, I would have thought.

A beat

Gill Sally, get the picture.
Sally I'm trying to.
Gill He makes me feel great! Christ how many men can you say that about?
Sally Well …

Gill No, honestly, how many? I wasn't born yesterday, you know that;
I know he could walk away and I'd be left looking like a fool, again.
How many times has that happened? But you know me, Sal, I've
always liked the fun of the fair: Spanish City, Alton Towers, you name
it, I'm there! It's the thrill of the ride!

Sally I can imagine.

Gill You have a got a bloody dirty mind, you have.

Sally Yes, listen who's talking!

Gill Sins of the flesh, Sal!

A beat

Sally Well you were right about one thing!

Gill What's that?

Sally He's different to the others.

Gill Listen I live in a bubble compared to some of the guys I've been
working with.

Sally So you are trying to save him?

A beat

Gill He's the only bloke I've been with who makes me feel good all the
time! He doesn't criticize, he takes me for who I am! He has never
said: "You don't look good in that, you look shit, your hair's a mess!
You're putting weight on!" He's the only bloke I've been with who
wants me on tap. And you know, I want him; how many men can you
actually say that about? Hey? Well all right I know it might not look
like a night at the Ritz, and I know it's early days, but I'll tell you
something Sal, it's real, this. It's as real as it gets for me, man!

Sally begins to cry. Gill awkwardly comforts her

Sally Oph, shit?

Gill Hey?

Sally You lucky sod!

Gill hugs Sally as she cries

Gill Hey, come on.

Sally I'm sorry!

Gill Hey, it's not that bad is it?

Sally Sometimes it is, Gill!

Gill Come on, babe...
Sally Oh you lucky, lucky sod!

Karl enters without a beer

Karl Oh, right. (*He stands watching and rubs his crotch*)

Gill strokes Sally's face

Gill Hey, hey!
Karl Oh, starting without me, eh?
Gill She's just letting it come out, that's all!

Karl realizes his misjudgement and grabs his bike

Karl There's a café along there and they've got a juke-box with some
old stuff on. We're splitting!
Sally (*still tearful*) I'm sorry! Oh dear!
Karl We're off!
Sally What about Mark?
Karl Fuck him, let him get lost. Only joking! Grab your bike, princess,
and we'll go over there. Come on, I'm starving, man!
Gill Hang on then, you!

*Gill and Karl head for the exit with their bicycles, leaving Sally
alone*

Mark enters with a bike

Gill and Karl freeze

Mark Right, so I'd walked about two miles pushing the damn bike; I'd
ruined my trousers, so that was my trousers and my shoes now! And
when I eventually caught up with them Sally was all over the shop. I
tell you, what a friggin' birthday!

Gill and Karl exit

Mark stops, holding his bike

Silence

Mark Is it far enough? I thought he'd kidnapped you!

Sally Where've you been?

Mark Chain came off! Got an adapter though, so I can get my phone charged.

A beat

Sally We're going to go for some lunch so ...

Mark Who says?

Sally Well, I'm starving, aren't you?

Mark Well, I am but my knee's killing me, can't we just have a minute?

Sally Well, Karl's found a café, so we'd better go!

Mark Why can't we leave them, they might fall in a canal and drown or something!

Sally Oh, don't!

Mark That was bloody stupid in the car. Why didn't you stop him!

Sally How?

Mark Haven't you got a mace spray? We could have had a bloody accident! Where've they gone?

Sally Just to a café!

Mark Come on then!

Sally attempts to stand but cannot manage it

Sally Oh hell!

Mark What's up?

Sally Oh ...

Mark You're probably stoned with all that smoke in the car.

Sally (*still on the floor*) Oh, I can't get up.

Mark Just get your bike ...

Sally Don't shout.

Mark I'm not shouting!

Sally (*appealing kindly*) You are!

Mark I'm not!

Sally You are, though!

Mark I'm not!

Sally You're being really heavy, though.

Mark I'm not!

Sally You are!

Mark No, I'm not!

Sally You are; you're being really heavy.

Mark I'm not being heavy.

Sally You are, you're really hassling me.

Mark Hassling you?

Sally Don't hassle me all right?

Mark (*sternly*) Sal, get the bike.

Sally (*still having problems!*) I cannot make my legs work! Do you understand? I can't make my friggin' legs work!

Mark considers the situation

Mark You haven't been drinking have you?

Sally All I've had all day is a bit of cake! I'm probably suffering malnutrition actually!

Mark Well, you've had more than me, I can tell you that.

Sally Karl gave me a piece; that is all I've been able to keep down since this morning!

A beat

Mark Oh, excellent!

Sally That is all I have had!

Mark What kind of cake was it?

Sally How do I know what kind of cake it was?

Mark Well, I bet it wasn't a Bakewell tart ...

Sally There you go, being heavy again!

Mark No, I am not being heavy.

Sally Man, you are!

Mark Saying it wasn't Bakewell tart is not getting heavy, I will get heavy in a minute, though.

Sally It was nice, actually.

Mark grabs Sally's bike and tries to help her get on it. Sally eventually gets to her feet. She tries to get hold of the bike during the following

Mark Get the bike ... Hold the bike, and let's get back to the hotel before it starts to rain. It's going to rain. Hold the bike! Have you got it?

Sally is all over the place but she now has hold of the bike

Sally I've got it!

Mark Right, get on!

Sally holds the bike but she is unable to cock her leg up to get on. She tries repeatedly but cannot swing her leg up. Mark is unimpressed but

Sally finds this hilarious. Mark simply looks at his wife in the realization that she is stoned

Sally I can't get my leg up … Shit! That's funny. Mark, that's funny. I can't get my leg over. Oh, don't look at me!
Mark What?
Sally Don't stare at me!
Mark I'm not staring at you!
Sally Oh, your face! Oh man, your face! And it had to be your chain that came off, didn't it? I'm sorry, but honestly … Oh, funny, man.
Mark Really?
Sally Oh I can't get my breath! (*She laughs outrageously*)
Mark (*losing his cool*) Get on the bloody bike!
Sally I can't get my leg up!
Mark You're pathetic.
Sally Your face, honestly!
Mark Give us it here. Where are they, over the road?

Mark snatches the bike from Sally and wheels both bikes off stage

Sally turns to the audience

Sally (*to the audience*) I couldn't believe they'd actually got me stoned! Me? Sally Thomas, Chair of the Village Hall Refurbishment Committee. If anybody knew, we wouldn't raise a penny! It wasn't exactly Woodstock but the last time I got off my head it was nineteen seventy-four and I got sun-stroke in Norwich and I was laid up for three days covered in lotion, and I looked like a mummy!

Mark enters pushing a piece of stage scenery, a frame representing a balcony

Mark (*to the audience*) Anyway, it was throwing it down when we got back to the hotel. I checked out my mum to see what was what! My dad said he couldn't believe I was fifty. He said fifty is the new thirty. Well, whoever believes that bollocks haven't seen me getting out of the bath! (*He adjusts the balcony setting into position*)
Sally I had a shower and a little nap but when I came to he was nowhere to be seen.
Mark I was stood on the hotel balcony, trying to get hold of my dad. It was just starting to rain and Sally was inside farting about with the TV — another mistake.

The Lights focus on the balcony

Disco music plays as if from a television

Sally goes US *of the balcony and turns her back on the audience*

Mark (*into the phone*) So she's stabilized — that's good then — and
how are you? ... You don't feel well either! ... Oh, that's not so good!
... No, you don't have to sing happy birthday, Dad! No, honestly ...

A beat

That's lovely, thanks very much! Very moving! I know you never miss
it! And I thank you for having me!
Sally (*calling; still with her back to the audience*) Mark?
Mark (*into the phone*) I'll have to go, Dad, Sally's shouting — I think
there must be a fire! We're back on the boat tomorrow night.
Sally Mark?
Mark (*into the phone*) Call me if you hear anything! ... OK, take it
steady, all right.

Mark looks at his phone and out towards the night during the following

Lights come up on Sally

Sally Have you seen this?
Mark I'm on the phone.
Sally Have you seen the telly?
Mark Why, what's up with it?
Sally There's nothing but porn. Come and have a look.
Mark I've just had my tea.
Sally Have you seen this lot?
Mark Why are you even looking?
Sally Mark?
Mark Turn it off.

A beat

Sally I think this is Karl!

A beat

Mark What?
Sally I think it's Karl on the telly!
Mark I wouldn't be surprised!

Sally He's on the telly.
Mark Is he waving?

A beat

Sally Waving what?

A beat

Mark Turn it off!
Sally Why?
Mark Turn it off!
Sally Oh, come and watch it with me, it's funny!
Mark I prefer Benny Hill!
Sally Oh, it is funny!
Mark No, it isn't!
Sally Oh, dear me!
Mark Turn it off or that telly's going out of the window!
Sally Come here a minute.
Mark (*to himself*) Why is it me ... ?
Sally Dear me!
Mark (*to the audience*) Now I know you might not believe this, but it's the truth. He was haunting me, and we hadn't even got near Springsteen yet, and that's what we'd come for!

The music stops. Sally joins Mark

Sally This is absolutely true! There was Karl in all his glory, with "Animal" tattooed on his bum and a bad moustache.
Mark And the soundtrack?
Sally (*to the audience*) That's all he was bothered about, he said the music didn't fit.
Mark (*to the audience*) They'd mixed a disco track with a medieval location, it just didn't work. Well it didn't!
Sally I mean I had intended to give Mark a birthday treat but he said he wasn't interested knowing Karl was technically in the room.

Mark and Sally reposition the frame onstage to represent the outside of the Casa Rossa Sex Show

Mark Anyway Boris had arranged to meet us inside a place called the Banana Bar!

Mark and Sally remain where they are

I think he was doing this just to wind us up.

Sally And if you haven't got an idea of what the Banana Bar's about you've got no imagination.

Mark Not that you need one when you get in there — it's like television, all the work's done for you!

Sally We only stayed in for one banana, didn't we?

Mark Bananas? It was like being in the bloody jungle!

Sally No, if that's the height of sophistication I'm happy enough raising money for a new roof in the village!

Mark Well, of course they didn't show up, did they? And we ended up waiting for them outside this live sex show called the Casa Rossa.

Sally It was like being in a spy film, wasn't it? People kept sliding up to us asking if we wanted to see live sex. He asked if they'd got any dead sex and they went away thinking we were perverts!

Mark So there we are, right, hanging about like we've got a deal to do!

Scene 5

Casa Rosso Sex Show

The Lights change

Music plays

Sally and Mark are less than happy. They hover nervously outside the Casa Rossa Sex Show

Sally Is this the right one?

Mark I think so!

Sally I don't know if I fancy it to be honest.

Mark Well, why didn't you say something?

Sally Why didn't you?

A beat

Mark Well, you'd better tell 'em then!

Sally Why don't you tell 'em?

Mark Would you want to, if he'd tried to break your neck?

Karl and Gill enter, calmly excited

Karl Aaaargh, they're here, look! Mucky sods!

Gill We were in the Banana Bar — didn't see you?

Sally Well, we were in there!

Karl Best show in Amsterdam this!

Sally That's good, then!

Karl You'll not believe your eyes!

A beat

Sally Well, actually, Karl … !

Karl What?

Sally Well …

Karl What's up?

Sally Well, erm …

Karl It's a right laugh in here — and I tell you sommat, they've got air-conditioning. Mind you, you need it! There'll be steam coming out your head!

Sally Well I don't think it's for me actually?

A beat

Karl What?

Sally I don't think it's for me!

Karl Why not?

Sally Well we've done the Banana Bar and I think we've got the picture!

Mark She's not been so well since you got her stoned — —

Sally I've not felt brilliant all day, actually, and it's going to be a long night, isn't it?

Karl It's him, he doesn't want to go in, feels shown up … It's nowt, man, don't worry about it! Nobody's hung like these lads!

Gill Karl's bent over backwards to get these tickets, you know!

Mark Well, he's in the right place for that!

Karl Tha what?

Mark He's in the right place for that!

Karl Oh, he's trying to be funny naa, look?

Mark Well, I have my moments!

Karl Well, tha's been making skits all weekend, so what are you saying?

Mark Well, I don't want to go any further down the plug hole, let's just say that!

Karl You what?

Mark Sally's not feeling well so I think we'll leave it!

Karl She looks all right to me! So why doesn't thy fuck off back to hotel if tha's not keen? Come on, Sally, you'll love it, let him go!

Sally (*to Mark; pressurized*) Well, shall we, just give it a go?

Mark I thought you didn't feel well?

Sally Well I don't want to cause a scene!

Mark Let's go back then!

Sally Well is it fair!

Mark If you're not well, let's go back!

A beat

Karl I mean, this is my treat and you're throwing kindness back in my face!

Mark Well, I'm sorry you feel like that about it!

Karl So am I, bud!

Mark (*to Gill*) Do you want to go in, Gill?

Gill Well, I can't see what the big deal is!

Mark No, right!

Gill Come on, I thought you fancied a bit of this, Mark!

Sally Well, he's always talking about it!

Gill I thought you fancied a threesome?

Karl There's all sorts in here, it's great!

Mark (*to Sally*) Well, do you feel well enough or what, it's your call?

Sally Well, I don't … !

Mark Do you want to go in or what?

Sally Well, if he's got the tickets!

Mark I thought you felt off it, though?

Karl Look straight in now — half an hour and then to the gig!

Sally Shall we?

Mark Well, you go in, then, but it's not for me!

Karl makes to depart; he turns and Gill makes to peel off with him

Karl He isn't going to like owt I like, coz he doesn't like me fucking anyway.

Mark No, you're right there!

Karl And he's answering back naa, look?

Mark You what?

Karl Is thy answering back?

Mark Yes, I am!

Karl And tha's staring again look, what have I told thee?

Mark I've had enough of this!

Karl Enough of what? We've done nowt yet. Just getting warmed up!

Mark Walking about like a Social Services outing!
Karl What's tha saying?
Mark Let's not go there, mate!
Karl I'm not thy mate, I've teld thee.
Mark Fine!
Karl Gill's teld me all about thee, tha knows!
Mark Has she?

The two men start to stand up to each other

Sally (*wanting out; to Mark*) Look, you go in and we'll see you afterwards!
Mark You should have tried harder at school; then I might have liked you then!
Sally (*becoming anxious*) Just ignore him, Karl. I'm sorry, Gill, it's not going to work out!
Karl I'm gunna fucking knock thee out in a minute!
Mark It was kids like you who waved their knobs at me during my piano lessons.
Karl I didn't even know thy had piano lessons!
Mark I've got my mother in hospital and this is the last thing I want!
Sally Hey come on, people are looking!
Mark Oh, ay, you can pay to see live sex but you can't have an argument in the street!
Sally (*panicking*) This is supposed to be a good weekend!
Karl I'm trying to give you a good weekend but you're too tight-arsed to enjoy it! When in Rome!
Sally We're not in Rome, though are we? I've been to Rome — it's not like this, actually!
Gill Oh, come on, Mark — don't spoil it!
Mark Don't spoil it? Oh hell! You spoilt it, when you got on the friggin' boat with Boris!
Gill It's Karl!
Mark I know who it is!
Karl Who's Boris?
Sally Mark, leave it!
Mark After all I've done for you?
Karl Who's Boris?
Gill I never asked for a penny!
Mark You never said no!
Karl Who's Boris?
Sally What are you on about?
Gill Doesn't Sally know?

Karl Who's this fucking Boris?

Mark It's my money!

Gill Oh, here we go — —

Karl Who's this Boris?

Sally What've you been doing?

Mark (*to Sally*) I've sent her money. I've tried to help her out that's all! And this is what she does to us!

Sally When?

Gill (*disbelievingly*) Oh God!

Mark I've paid her rent!

Karl Hey up, Gill, who's this fucking Boris?

Mark I've paid for her holidays!

Sally When?

Mark For the last three years.

Sally Why?

Mark I paid for her to go to Malaga last March.

Gill (*to Sally*) I thought you knew!

Karl Why didn't you tell me about him?

Mark And she never even sent us a card!

Sally And we're saving to send the kids private?

Mark And now she turns up with Boris the circus act and I'm expected to pay for him!

Karl Hey, listen, I don't know a Boris, but if I find out he's got owt to do with Gill he's friggin dead!

Mark After all I've tried to do! I mean the crossing, the hotel, I even had to pay a cancellation fee on the restaurant!

Karl steps away to return a thought

Karl Yes now then, I'll tell you sommat about that hotel, shall I? It's fucking freezing in our room! Isn't it?

Gill It is, we were going to complain weren't we?

Karl Yes, we were, but we didn't because we're trying to be all right with you!

A beat

Sally We'll see you at the concert, shall we? Shall we do that? Shall we see you there, this is just daft it's been such a good weekend it's a shame to spoil it!

Mark Oh, a good weekend?

A beat

Karl I'll tell thee sommat, tha doesn't like me, well I don't fucking like you! I didn't like thee from the moment I met thee on the boat! Tha's been trying to stay with me all weekend, but you can't because I'm better than thee at everything! And I don't like what tha's been doing to Gill. You can't buy people, mate! So what have you got to say about that?

Mark Up yours, mate!

Karl I'm not your mate, and I never will be!

Mark Good!

Karl I could eat you!

Mark Only if I let you!

There is a stand-off

Karl You don't know how to enjoy yoursens! Show'll have started now; and I hate missing the beginning.

Karl exits into the sex club

Silence

Gill (*in tears*) I just — can't believe the way you're treating me. (*To Sally*) I never asked him for money. (*To Mark*) I've never asked you for anything, just to be a mate! And now you can't even do that! Who the friggin' hell do you think you are? Well, I'll tell you something — stick your house and kids up your arse!

Gill exits into the club

Mark calls after Gill as she goes (WHAT DOES HE SAY?)

Silence

Sally How long have you been sending her money?

Mark Oh, don't!

Sally Why didn't you tell me what were you after?

Mark I was just trying to help her!

Sally (*close to tears*) Oh, give up! I don't know if I'm having withdrawal symptoms from the dope, or I need a joint, but I feel bloody depressed.

A beat

We could have just gone in and saved all this upset!
Mark I thought you didn't want to go in?
Sally I didn't.
Mark Well, shut up, then!

Mark exits

Sally (*to the audience*) Honestly, arguing in the street? There was a bigger crowd around us than there were around some of the hookers! A group of Norwegians thought it was a piece of street theatre and they wouldn't let us alone till we got back to the hotel!

Mark enters

Mark (*picking up the narration*) I don't know to this day what happened in the Casa Rosso and I don't know what state Gill and Karl were in when they came back from the concert — but I've got a good imagination!

Black-out

The music fades

SCENE 6

Hotel Lobby

The chairs and table from the boat in Act I have been re-set as the furniture of the hotel lobby

The Lights come up. Karl and Gill, out of their heads, are slumped in the chairs

Piano music filters through underneath the scene

Karl "Glory Days"!
Gill "Thunder Road"!
Karl As an encore. Man he is boss!
Gill He's the boss man!

A beat

Karl and Gill sing the first verse of Bruce Springsteen's 'Streets of Philadelphia'

A beat

Gill Enjoyed it?
Karl It was good of them to let me come wasn't it?

Gill starts to giggle

What happened to Mark and Sally?
Gill Didn't see them!
Karl Probably gone to that sex show when we came out.
Gill Good show ...
Karl I've done that!
Gill So have I!
Karl Where?
Gill Everywhere ...
Karl (*giggling*) That's funny man ... That's funny ...
Gill Kiss me ...

He does so

Karl I love you, doll!
Gill Do you?
Karl I love you, man!
Gill Woman.
Karl Whatever ...
Gill It's been a good weekend.

A beat

Karl Tomorrow we'll do the sights and you know what I might do, I
  might throw him off the boat.
Gill Oh, I forgot to give him his present.
Karl What did you get him?
Gill They're here — I was going to give 'em him at the concert. (*She
  reveals a pair of handcuffs which have a sexual connotation*)
Karl Oh, officer!
Gill What?
Karl Arrest me!
Gill Arrest me.
Karl You don't know how funny that is!

Karl and Gill stand, still giggling

Neil Diamond's "Red Red Wine" plays

Karl and Gill exit

The Lights cross-fade to the Sky Lounge setting and the music fades

   Sally enters

We are back in the Sky Lounge

Sally (*to the audience*) We got back after the argument and sat on the bed for half an hour, not speaking. And I'd like to say it was typical of us, but you'll never believe what we did then! I think a lot of this was about Mark being fifty but I suppose that's what makes him who he is.

Mark enters with a chilled bottle of champagne and two glasses for himself and Sally. He places them on the table

Mark (*to the audience*) The daft thing was — we didn't even see the Springsteen gig!

Sally No, can you believe it? We raided the mini-bar, packed our bags and checked out of the hotel.

Mark I cancelled my credit card on Boris' and Gill's room. Said it had been a mistake

Sally And we set off for Antwerp!

Mark It was all very rock 'n' roll!

Sally I thought it was a lousy trick but Mark left Karl a little note, didn't you, what did it say?

Mark It was nothing — it just said "Fuck you!"

Sally Isn't that awful?

Mark It was from the heart of my bottom!

Sally Then we travelled down to Antwerp — but we couldn't find a hotel to stay in.

Mark Well, it was Saturday night!

Sally So we stuck some music on and we drove to Bruges!

Mark Couldn't get in there!

Sally No room at the inn!

Mark So we came all the way back through the chunnel!

Sally Drinking the stuff we'd got from the mini bar!

Mark We got to Hythe, music blasting out of the car. Couldn't get in a hotel!

Sally So we slept in the car, on the sea front, like two teenagers.

Mark Couldn't walk in the morning, could we?

Sally Looked like death warmed up.

Mark But I'd an idea for the kid's thing I was doing!

Sally So he was in a better mood!

Mark And my mum had gone on to a ward, so she was being sorted out!

Sally But my dad had had an angina do. Fixing the greenhouse!

Mark So he was in A and E!

Sally Hey, listen, you can't write this!

A beat

Mark I mean I'd always had this thing about Gill.

Sally Well, that had been put to bed!

Mark But Karl had brought something out of me!

Sally Yes, basically, Karl was a skinhead and he's an old rocker really — they were never going to get on!

Mark Yes, I'd forgotten that.

Sally Fancy driving all the way back from Amsterdam drunk and singing Springsteen songs. We need sectioning!

Mark And Karl and Gill didn't last, did it?

Sally She'd got an advert for a German insurance company. Met a bloke in Frankfurt, five months later. Broke Karl's heart apparently!

Mark Gill kept kissing Karl but he never turned into a prince.

Sally Well, I've been doing that for twenty-five years and look at you!

Mark I knew she was going to say that!

Sally And you can please yourselves, but we think it is getting worse, so we don't go out much — we stay on our island! That's why we're happy in the Sky Lounge.

Mark And I realized, you see, how much I was in love with Sal.

Sally But he never says it!

Mark I was even in love with her dad for a short time!

Sally But that didn't last!

Mark And we're happy to cruise through life now!

Sally Just as long as it's smooth.

A beat

Mark Well, here we are then!

Sally Sat in the Sky Lounge!

Mark On the *Pride of Hull*!

Sally And a crooner's been singing Neil Diamond!

Mark But down in the disco —

Sally — they're playing Bruce Springsteen.

A beat

Mark We're going down in a minute!
Sally We're not, are we?
Mark We are!

Mark takes a big drink. He and Sally toast the audience

Bruce Springsteen's "Born to Run" plays

The Lights fade to Black-out

CURTAIN

FURNITURE AND PROPERTY LIST

ACT I
SCENE 1

On stage: Small round table
Two chairs

Off stage: SCENE 2 Sun Deck setting

SCENE 2

Personal: **Gill**: cigarettes and lighter

SCENE 3

Off stage: Drinks (**Mark**)

SCENE 4

No additional properties

SCENE 5

ANY EXTRA SET ITEMS FOR THIS SCENE?

Off stage: Cocktail

Personal: **Gill**: cigarettes and lighter

SCENE 6

Off stage: Drink (**Sally**)

SCENE 7

Set: Empty glasses on table

Off stage: Drinks (**Gill**)
Drinks (**Karl**)

SCENE 8

Off stage: Large truck of cabin doorframe (**Mark**)

SCENE 9

No additional properties

SCENE 10

Personal: **Mark**: mobile phone
               Karl: joint-making materials

ACT II
SCENE 1

Strike: Sky Lounge chairs and table

Off stage: Small car with sick bag (**Mark**)

SCENE 2

No additional properties

SCENE 3

Off stage: Bicycle (**Sally**)

SCENE 4

Off stage: 3 bicycles (**Karl, Gill, Mark**)
               Truck with frame representing balcony (**Mark**)

Personal: **Karl**: piece of space cake wrapped in tinfoil

SCENE 5

No additional properties

SCENE 6

Set: Chairs and table from ACT I

Off stage: Chilled bottle of champagne and two glasses (**Mark**)

Personal: **Gill**: handcuffs

LIGHTING PLOT

Practical fittings required: festoon lights
Various simple settings

ACT I, SCENE 1

To open: Darkness

Cue 1	Introduction to "Hello Again" plays (Page 1) *Bring up lights on Sky Lounge setting*	
Cue 2	**Mark**: "And a crooner is singing Neil Diamond!" *Bring up spotlight on Singer*	(Page 1)
Cue 3	**Mark** and **Sally** politely applaud *Fade spotlight on Singer*	(Page 2)

ACT I, SCENE 2

Cue 4	When ready *Cross-fade lights to sun deck setting*	(Page 8)

ACT I, SCENE 3

Cue 5	When ready *Cross-fade lights to Sky Lounge setting*	(Page 12)
Cue 6	Introduction leads into song *Bring up spotlight on* **Singer**	(Page 12)
Cue 7	**Singer**: "Thank you!" *Fade spotlight on* **Singer**	(Page 12)
Cue 8	**Singer** exits *Bring up lights on* **Sally** *and* **Gill**	(Page 12)
Cue 9	**Gill** exits *Fade lights to Blackout*	(Page 20)

ACT I, Scene 4

| *Cue* 10 | When ready | (Page 20) |
| | *Bring up lights on Sky Lounge setting* | |

ACT I, Scene 5

| *Cue* 11 | When ready | (Page 21) |
| | *Cross-fade lights to Irish Bar setting* | |

| *Cue* 12 | Mark sits in the Sky Lounge | (Page 32) |
| | *Fade lights to Black-out* | |

ACT I, Scene 6

| *Cue* 13 | When ready | (Page 32) |
| | *Bring up spotlight on* **Mark** *and dim light on rest of stage* | |

| *Cue* 14 | **Sally**: " … the ship's policeman still standing!" | |
| | *Fade lights to Black-out* | |

ACT I, Scene 7

| *Cue* 15 | When ready | (Page 33) |
| | *Bring up disco lighting* | |

ACT I, Scene 8

| *Cue* 16 | When ready | (Page 35) |
| | *Cross-fade lights to Sky Lounge setting* | |

ACT I, Scene 9

Cue 17	When ready	(Page 36)
	Tighten focus of lights on to cabin setting;	
	bring up festoon lights	

ACT I, Scene 10

| *Cue* 18 | When ready | (Page 39) |
| | *Change lights to indicate a bad storm* | |

| *Cue* 19 | Music | (Page 41) |
| | *Fade lights slowly* | |

| *Cue* 20 | **Mark** tries to get a signal on his phone | (Page 41) |
| | *Black-out* | |

ACT II, SCENE 1

Pre-set: General exterior lighting

Cue 21	When ready *Fade pre-set lights*	(Page 42)
Cue 22	**Sally** enters *Bring up general exterior lighting*	(Page 42)
Cue 23	**Mark** gets into the car *Focus lighting on car*	(Page 43)
Cue 24	**Mark**: " ... I will hit the roof." *Black-out*	(Page 51)

ACT II, SCENE 2

Cue 25	Music fades *Bring up lights on car with movement effect*	(Page 52)
Cue 26	**Mark** and **Sally** get out of the car *Fade lights to black-out*	(Page 58)

ACT II, SCENE 3

Cue 27	When ready *Bring up general exterior lighting*	(Page 58)

ACT II, SCENE 4

Cue 28	**Sally**: "It was almost pleasant, actually!" (Page 58) *Change lights to outdoor effect with lime tree gobo*

Cue 29	**Mark**: " — another mistake." *Focus lighting on the balcony*	(Page 67)
Cue 30	**Mark** looks at his phone *Bring up lights on Sally*	(Page 68)
Cue 31	**Mark**: " ... we've got a deal to do!" *Change lights to Casa Rosso setting*	(Page 70)
Cue 32	**Mark**: "— but I've got a good imagination!" *Black-out*	

ACT II, Scene 6

| *Cue* 33 | When ready
Bring up interior lights | (Page 76) |

Cue 33   When ready   (Page 76)
               Bring up interior lights

Cue 34   **Karl** and **Gill** exit   (Page 78)
               Cross-fade lights to Sky Lounge setting

Cue 35   Bruce Springsteen's "Born to Run" plays   (Page 80)
               Fade lights to black-out

EFFECTS PLOT

ACT I

Cue 14	**Mark**: " … like death warmed up!"	(Page 36)
	Howling wind	
Cue 15	Lights come up on ACT I, SCENE 9	(Page 36)
	Shake festoon lights	
Cue 16	Lights change to indicate bad storm	(Page 39)
	Shake festoon lights more. Sound of howling wind, fading	
Cue 17	**Mark**: " … until we got to Amsterdam."	(Page 41)
	Music: "Tomorrow Night" by Atomic Rooster	

ACT II

Cue 18	During interval	(Page 42)
	Music	
Cue 19	Lighting pre-set fades	(Page 42)
	Fade music	
Cue 20	**Mark** gets into the car	(Page 43)
	Low smoke; sound of ship's horn and ripple of water	
Cue 21	Black-out	(Page 51)
	Music: "Radar Love"	
Cue 22	When ready	(Page 52)
	Fade music to sound as if played over the car radio	
Cue 23	**Karl**: " … we're going to have a good time."	(Page 57)
	Segue music into "Dancing in the Dark", quietly	
Cue 24	**Karl** turns up the radio (Page 57)	
	Increase volume of music	
Cue 25	Lights come up on ACT II, SCENE 3	(Page 58)
	Fade music	
Cue 26	Lights change	(Page 60)
	Sounds of birds and barges	
Cue 27	The lights focus on the balcony	(Page 68)
	Disco music as if from a television	
Cue 28	**Mark**: " … and that's what we'd come for!"	(Page 69)
	Cut music	

COPYRIGHT MUSIC

Lightning Source UK Ltd.
Milton Keynes UK
UKOW01f0611310715

256123UK00001B/8/P